THE COMPANION STUDY

Redeeming Love

FRANCINE RIVERS

WITH ANGELA HUNT

MULTNOMAH

Details in some anecdotes and stories have been changed to protect the identities of the persons involved.

Trade Paperback ISBN 978-0-525-65436-0
eBook ISBN 978-0-525-65437-7

Printed in the United States of America on acid-free paper

waterbrookmultnomah.com

4 6 8 9 7 5 3

First Edition

CONTENTS

Introduction v

INTRODUCTION

It has long been a dream of mine to offer a companion Bible study to my novel *Redeeming Love*. The book is based on the biblical story of the prophet Hosea and his wife, Gomer, but bears a similarity to the path many of us take from brokenness to redemption and wholeness in Christ. Our culture portrays love as a feeling, but love is also an action. The primary character in *Redeeming Love* is Michael. His character shows what it means to love as Jesus did. Feelings swell and fade, but true love stands the test of time. It involves commitment and hard work and brings greater, longer-lasting blessings than we can imagine. Michael displayed Christ's love for Angel because he decided to see his wife through eyes of compassion, patience, virtue, and self-sacrifice. He was passionate for her. He took his marriage vows to heart, striving to bless her through their marriage.

This kind of love isn't just the stuff of storybooks. It is possible through the power of God given to every believer. Falling in love with someone is easy, but steadfast, passionate love that lasts for a lifetime is a matter of choice.

Angie Hunt and I agreed from the start that this project would not be like other Bible studies. Inside this book you will find three lessons per week, rather than the usual five, because we want you to ponder the concepts presented. We want you to take your time and look up scriptures to see how they apply to your life today.

Michael, Angel, and the other characters from *Redeeming Love* are fictional, but all the other people mentioned in this study lived and walked this earth. They were real people who can inspire us because they endured real trials. The Word of God is living and breathing and cuts to the heart of our lives (Hebrews 4:12). It shows us the blessed way to walk purposefully and with joy. In these lessons you will see that truth in how God worked in individual lives.

This is not a fill-in-the-blank study. We hope you will invest in a notebook and write whatever thoughts, feelings, observations, and prayers come to you as you read. We also hope you underline and highlight passages, jot notes in the margins, and turn your study book into a dog-eared, much-used resource and reference for your journey. Please don't stop with what we've offered. The Bible is full of history, wisdom, and applicable lessons for you. You'll discover victims who became victors, the lost who were found, the hurting who were healed, and the dead who rose to life. The Bible tells God's story through each book of history.

What Angie and I want most is for you to know personally the God who loves you with an all-consuming, cleansing fire, the God who designed you and knows the special plans He has for you (Jeremiah 29:11). Our heartfelt prayer is that you will open your mind and heart to Him. If you do, He will make you new and more alive than you've ever been.

May the Lord bless you and keep you as you read His Word. May He shine His face on you, reveal Himself to you, and give you peace (Numbers 6:24–26).

One

CHILD OF DARKNESS

MY CHILDHOOD WAS NOT like Angel's. I had loving parents who believed in God. Our family attended church every Sunday. I went to Sunday school, summer camp, and youth group and thought I was a Christian. When I went away to college, I stopped attending church. It was the sixties revolution. No one told me that anything "free" still costs dearly. And so free love cost my innocence, my self-respect, and a baby's life. I thought I could just pick up the pieces of my life and move on.

When I had just about hit rock bottom, I received a letter from an old hometown friend, Rick Rivers, serving in the Marine Corps in Vietnam. We started to correspond. Once he came home, we dated, fell in love, and married a year later. Though Rick came from a solid, loving family, he knew nothing about Christianity other than what his grandmother had taught him: Psalm 23 and the Lord's Prayer. I didn't know until years later that he had an encounter with God during the 1968 Tet Offensive in Vietnam. It would be many more years until he gave his life to Christ.

We both had burdens weighing heavily on our hearts and souls, baggage we carried into our marriage. We had high and low times. I suffered from my past mistakes. Rick suffered from war memories and alcohol abuse. We loved and fought each other, and it all came down to one question for both of us individually: Who is in control of my life?

Looking back, I realize God placed many people in our lives to draw us to Him. We kept ignoring the pull, mistakenly believing we could figure things out ourselves. The turning point came when Rick decided to start his own business and we sold our home and moved closer to family. We experienced stressful outer changes but no inner changes. I waited in Southern California until our three young children finished the school year, while Rick moved north, lived with his parents, and set up business in Sebastopol. He hunted for a rental home for our family. Only one was available—situated between two Christian families, both of whom invited us to church within hours of our moving in.

Our marriage was crumbling, and I was desperate enough to try anything—even God—to stop the pain. "Seek, and you will find," the Scriptures say (Matthew 7:7, NASB), and faith in Jesus came to me in our neighbors' church. Rick found Christ later, in our home Bible study taught by the pastor.

The gospel of Jesus Christ opened our hearts and poured life into our souls. The book of Hosea opened my eyes to the truth. Whenever I'd had a problem, the Lord was the last one I would seek out for answers. I'd lived as a child of darkness until I was in my late thirties. I had been like Gomer, prostituting myself to worldly ideas and practices that defied God and left deep wounds. Now I recognize His loving hand on me from the time I was born. He was always near. In every tempting and potentially life-damaging situation, God had offered a way of escape. I chose not to take it. Even so, God never stopped loving me. And now that I walk with Jesus, He has used what Satan meant for my destruction for His good purpose, not only in my life but also in the lives of others. He can do the same for you.

Light and Shadows

*There are some things that once you've lost,
you never get back. Innocence is one. Love is another.
I guess childhood is a third.*

JOHN MARSDEN, *CHECKERS*

ALEX BENT DOWN *to Sarah. "I want you to go outside and play," he
said quietly. "I want to talk to your mother alone." He smiled and
patted her cheek.*

*Sarah smiled, utterly enchanted. Papa had touched her; he wasn't
angry at all. He loved her! Just as Mama said. "Can I come back when
you're done talking?"*

*Papa straightened stiffly. "Your mother will come and get you when
she's ready. Now, run along as you've been told."*

*"Yes, Papa." Sarah wanted to stay, but she wanted to please her
father more. She went out of the parlor, skipping through the kitchen
to the back door. She picked a few daisies that grew in the garden
patch by the door and then headed for the rose trellis. She plucked the
petals. "He loves me, he loves me not, he loves me, he loves me not . . ."
She hushed as she came around the corner. She didn't want to disturb
Mama and Papa. She just wanted to be close to them.*

*Sarah dreamed contentedly. Maybe Papa would put her up on his
shoulders. She wondered if he would take her for a ride on his big*

black horse. She would have to change her dress, of course. He wouldn't want her to soil it. She wished he had let her sit on his lap while he talked to Mama. She would have liked that very much, and she would have been no bother.

The parlor window was open, and she could hear voices. Mama loved the smell of roses to fill the parlor. Sarah wanted to sit and listen to her parents. That way she would know just when Papa wanted her to come back again. If she was very quiet, she wouldn't disturb them, and all Mama would have to do was lean out and call her name.

"What was I to do, Alex? You've never spent so much as a minute with her. What was I to tell her? That her father doesn't care? That he wishes she had never even been born?"

Sarah's lips parted. Deny it, Papa! Deny it!

"You know how I feel about her."

"How can you say how you feel? You don't even know her. She's a beautiful child, Alex. She's quick and charming and she isn't afraid of anything. She's like you in so many ways. She's someone, *Alex. You can't ignore her existence forever. She's your daughter . . ."*

"I have enough children by my wife. Legitimate children. I told you I didn't want another."

"How can you say that? How can you not love your own flesh and blood?"

"I told you how I felt from the beginning, but you wouldn't listen. She should never have been born, Mae, but you insisted on having your own way."

"Do you think I wanted to get pregnant? Do you think I planned to have her?"

"I've often wondered. Especially when I arranged a way out of the situation for you and you refused. The doctor I sent you to would have taken care of the whole mess. He would've gotten rid—"

"I couldn't do it. How could you expect me to kill my unborn child? Don't you understand? It's a mortal sin."

"You've spent too much time in church," he said derisively. *"Have you ever thought that you wouldn't have the problems you do now if you had gotten rid of her the way I told you. It would've been easy. But you ran out. Did you have her because you thought bearing my child would give you a hold over me you otherwise lacked?"*

"You can't believe that!" Mama was crying now.

"And how much time do I have left with you today? Enough? You've used it up on her. I told you what would happen, didn't I? I wish she had never been born!"

As the story of Angel opened, we met Sarah, the pretty little girl who lived with her mama in a small house surrounded by flowers. Sarah was not only cute but also bright, brave, and innocent, though her innocence was shattered all too quickly. She knew she had a father, and her mama said he was handsome. She also saw his fabulous gifts, which Mama passed on to Sarah, explaining they came from her papa.

Sarah had to wait to meet her father. Finally Mama thought she was old enough, so Sarah donned her loveliest dress and took pains to keep it clean. She tried her best to be charming, polite, and sweet—all to win her father's approval.

But all too quickly she overheard that her father didn't love her, didn't want her, and wished she had never been born. He considered her a mistake.

When we begin our lives, we spring fresh and blameless from the hand of God. We are born with willful human natures, true, but in our early years most of us are loved, carefully supervised, and given all the affection we need to thrive.

The world is a big mystery to us, but we eagerly explore it. And it doesn't take long before we test the limits our parents give us. As toddlers, two of our favorite words are *no* and *mine*. We want what we want. Little do we know we will spend the rest of our lives dealing with our stubborn, frustrating desires.

The Bible begins with a story of innocence too. In the first chapter, we read that God created the world and filled it with beauty—light and night, heavens above and earth below, the seas and dry land, plants and trees, the sun, the moon, stars to show the seasons, fish, birds, insects, animals, and people—each living thing producing *offspring of the same kind.* Notice how that phrase is repeated several times. God reassures His children that they didn't come crawling out of the sludge.

God molded man out of the earth, but He created woman from a part of man. Woman is flesh and bone of man. I like that. God breathed life into humankind. Only a breath separates us from Him. He gave us, quite literally, the breath of life. Without breath, we cannot live.

God placed His first humans in the beautiful Eden and taught them how to tend it. Two trees grew in the center of the garden: the tree of life and the tree of the knowledge of good and evil. "From all the trees of the garden," God said, "you are most welcome to eat. But of the Tree of the Knowledge of Good and Evil you must not eat" (Genesis 2:16–17, TLV). That command was the *only* law God gave them.

Those first two people, Adam and Eve, thrived in their innocence. They reveled in the beauty of nature; they explored their new bodies; they talked with God and learned how to care for their amazing home. Naked before Him and each other, they had no shame. They had nothing to hide from God or from each other.

And then . . . evil reared its head in the form of a serpent. This was an old evil, a fallen angel who had rebelled against God. He took on the form of a snake and slithered into the garden, daring to approach Eve. His subtle questioning made her doubt God's intent, and in that moment she stopped believing that God's way was the best. As Adam stood close by, silent, she trusted the serpent's word over God's single command and ate from the forbidden tree. When she offered the forbidden fruit to her husband, Adam took and ate it. Eve was deceived, and Adam chose to follow her lead.

That evening, God went into the garden to walk and talk in fellowship with the man and woman. Adam and Eve understood why He had told them not to eat from the tree of the knowledge of good and evil. The moment they disregarded God's protective command in favor of Satan's lies, their innocence disappeared. And now they hid from the One who loved them. When He called, they went reluctantly, inhabited by sin, guilty and ashamed, willing to offer excuses, unwilling to confess. By their choice, they had separated themselves from God.

> Then the LORD God said, "Look, the human beings have become like us, knowing both good and evil. What if they reach out, take fruit from the tree of life, and eat it? Then they will live forever!" (3.22)

God expelled Adam and Eve from the garden so they would not eat of the tree that gave eternal life—probably because He didn't want them to live eternally in a sinful state. Adam lived 930 years, but now seventy years are allotted to humankind, even longer if we are especially blessed (Psalm 90:10). Perhaps our shorter life span is a mercy. As I grow older, I know I'm getting closer to going home, and I'm okay with that.

As descendants of Adam and Eve, we inherited their nature, including their inclination to make decisions that separate us from God and continue to cause us, as well as others, great suffering. One decision separated us, but one decision can also reestablish that love relationship, though not yet in the same physical way Adam and Eve experienced it in the garden.

Little Sarah's innocence vanished the moment she realized her mother's word could not be trusted. Mama had implied that Sarah's father loved her, and Sarah had dreamed of him for as long as she could remember. What a shattering moment to learn that Alex not only despised her but also had wanted to destroy her before birth.

Alex's admission rocked Sarah's world, and his dark heart continued to bear destructive fruit in his innocent daughter's life.

TO THINK ABOUT

1. Can you remember a moment in your life when your innocence was destroyed? What was the situation? How did you feel afterward? In that moment did you learn that someone you loved was untrustworthy?

2. How did you feel about Sarah after reading this part of the prologue? She had so many positive qualities: brightness, beauty, and bravery. She sought to please her mother and father. She yearned for a complete family. How did this scene make you root for this little girl?

3. Milton wrote his famous work *Paradise Lost* about the Garden of Eden. Have you ever thought of the Adam and Eve account (found in Genesis 3) as a tale of innocence lost?

4. The John Marsden quote says innocence, love, and childhood can never be regained. Speaking of childhood, the old song "Toyland" says, "Once you pass its borders, you can ne'er return again."[1] Can innocence be regained?

5. Today's children, even babies, are often subjected to sounds, images, and experiences that were not commonly encountered by children of past generations. Children are losing their innocence at increasingly younger ages. What can we do to reverse this unfortunate situation?

One day some parents brought their little children to Jesus so he could touch and bless them. But when the disciples saw this, they scolded the parents for bothering him.

Then Jesus called for the children and said to the disciples, "Let the children come to me. Don't stop them! For the Kingdom of God belongs to those who are like these children. I tell you the truth, anyone who doesn't receive the Kingdom of God like a child will never enter it." (Luke 18:15–17)

Children love openly and honestly. Sarah felt that way about her papa, even though she'd never met him face to face. We come to Jesus in the same manner, with open and honest hearts, with no pretense and no hidden motives. He knows all about us and loves us anyway. He forgives our wrongdoings and enfolds us in His grace.

As you go through the rest of your day, talk to Jesus as simply as a child would. No need for fancy theological words or traditional phrases with Him. Just speak from your heart and listen for His reply.

Come close to God, and God will come close to you. (James 4:8)

Darkness and Despair

Darkness cannot drive out darkness; only light can do that. Hate cannot drive out hate; only love can do that.
MARTIN LUTHER KING JR., *STRENGTH TO LOVE*

WHEN THEY ARRIVED *home, Mama pretended everything was fine, but Sarah knew something was terribly wrong. There were boxes out, and Mama was packing her things.*

"We're going to visit your grandmother and grandfather," Mama said brightly, but her eyes looked dull and dead. "They've never seen you." She told Cleo she was sorry to dismiss her, and Cleo said that was fine. She had decided to marry Bob, the butcher, after all. Mama said she hoped Cleo would be very happy, and Cleo went away.

Sarah awakened in the middle of the night. Mama wasn't in the bed, but Sarah could hear her. She followed the sound of her mother's stricken voice and went into the parlor. The window was open, and she went to look out. What was Mama doing outside in the middle of the night?

Moonlight flowed over the flower garden and Sarah saw her mother kneeling in her thin white nightgown. She was ripping all the flowers out. Handful after handful, she yanked the plants up and flung them in all directions, weeping and talking to herself as she did. She picked up a knife and came to her feet. She went down again on her knees beside her beloved rose bushes. One after another, she cut the roots. Every last one of them.

Then she bent forward and sobbed, rocking herself back and forth, back and forth, the knife still in her hand.

SHE DIED IN *the morning, the first sunlight of spring on her face and her rosary beads in her dead-white hands. Rab wept violently, but Sarah had no tears. The heaviness inside her seemed almost too great to bear. When Rab went out for a while, she lay down beside Mama and put her arms around her.*

Mama was so cold and stiff. Sarah wanted to warm her. Sarah's eyes felt gritty and hot. She closed them and whispered over and over, "Wake up, Mama. Wake up. Please, wake up." When she didn't, Sarah couldn't stop the tears. "I want to go with you. Take me, too. God, please, I want to go with my mama." She wept until exhaustion overtook her and only awakened when Rab lifted her away from the bed. Men were with him.

The men talked as though she weren't there. Maybe she wasn't anymore. Maybe she was different, the way Mama once said.

"I bet Mae was real pretty once," one said as he began sewing the shroud closed over Mama's face.

"She's better off dead," Rab said, crying again. "At least now she's not unhappy. She's free."

Free, *Sarah thought.* Free of me. If I hadn't been born, Mama would live in a nice cottage in the country with flowers all around. Mama would be happy. Mama would be alive.

"Wait a minute," said one, and pried the rosary from Mama's fingers and dropped it in Sarah's lap. "I bet she woulda wanted you to have that, honey." He finished the stitching while Sarah ran the beads through her cold fingers and stared at nothing.

She remembered Mama's going to the big church and talking to the man in black. He talked a long time, and Mama had listened, her head bowed, tears running down her cheeks. Mama never went back, but sometimes she would still sift the beads through her slender fingers while the rain spat on the window.

"What good are you?!" Sarah screamed again. "Tell me!"

WHEN THE MAN *let go of her, she ran to the farthest corner of the room and cowered there. He stood in the middle of the room looking at her for a long time. Then he went to the marble stand and poured water into the porcelain bowl. He wrung out a white cloth and walked toward her. She pressed back as far as she could. He hunkered down and grasped her chin.*

"You're much too pretty for paint," he said and began to wash her face.

She shuddered violently at his touch. She looked at the place where Rab had lain. The man tipped her chin back.

"I don't think that drunken lout was your father. You don't look anything like him, and there's intelligence in your eyes." He finished washing the rouge from her cheeks and mouth and tossed the cloth aside. "Look at me, little one."

When Sarah did, her heart pounded until her whole body shook with terror.

He held her face so she couldn't look away. "As long as you do exactly what I tell you to do, we're going to get along fine." He smiled faintly and stroked her cheek, his eyes glowing strangely. "What's your name?"

Sarah couldn't answer.

He touched her hair, her throat, her arm. "It doesn't matter. I think I'm going to call you Angel." Straightening, he took her hand. "Come on now, Angel. I have things to teach you." He lifted her and *sat her on the big bed. "You can call me Duke, when you get your tongue back." He took off his black silk coat. "Which you will. Shortly." He smiled again as he removed his tie and slowly began to unbutton his shirt.*

And by morning, Sarah knew that Cleo had told her God's truth about everything.

❦

When Sarah's father abandoned Mae because she would not disown her daughter, Mae was forced to earn a living any way she could. She sold her belongings, moved to cheaper housing, and finally resorted to prostitution. She then took up with Rab, an alcoholic who had a kind heart but could not cope with the responsibilities of parenthood when Mae died. After hearing that a wealthy man was looking for a young girl to adopt, Rab took Sarah to meet the man, despite a stern warning from the madam at the brothel where Rab was to meet the mysterious Duke.

Duke had Rab murdered and proceeded to "teach" Sarah—while shattering her innocence and breaking her spirit.

Duke annihilated Sarah's joyful childhood, leaving her in emotional and spiritual darkness. By the time the sun rose again, Sarah was no more, and the broken girl on the bed had a new name, Angel, and a far different future than her mama had imagined for her.

Throughout history, other young girls have had their dreams destroyed in an instant. In ancient Persia, during the reign of King Xerxes, a young Jewish girl, Hadassah, lived with her cousin. She was not unacquainted with sorrow, for her parents had died, but she fully expected to marry a young Jewish man, raise children, and follow the customs of her people. Like Sarah, Hadassah was exceptionally beautiful.

In 483 BC, King Xerxes threw a massive party that lasted half a year. On the final night, his wife, Vashti, refused to appear at his command, and he removed her as queen. History tells us that a few years later, he suffered a disastrous defeat in the war against the Greeks. When he returned to his palace and yearned for a woman's comfort, he remembered Vashti and what he had done. Some of his advisers suggested he take a new wife, perhaps to distract him from despair. Instead of searching for lovely young girls among the Persian nobility, they threw out a larger net, conducting a search-and-seize campaign for beauties to add to the king's harem. Some have described this event as a royal beauty pageant, but it was not voluntary. Attractive young girls were taken, willing or not, confined to the royal palace, and considered the king's property.

Hadassah was one of the captive girls. Taken from her cousin's home, she was placed in the royal palace and forced to endure a year of beauty treatments. The House of the Virgins may not sound like a tough gig, but slavery in a gilded cage is still slavery. The Persians worshipped a pagan god named Ahura Mazdā, while the Jews worshipped Adonai and kept a strict religious law given to them by Moses. Hadassah, a devout young woman, had been warned by her cousin to keep quiet about her religious heritage, so she could not always avoid forbidden foods or practices. She was also given a new name: Hadassah became known as Esther, a Persian word for "star."

The girl who had likely dreamed of marrying a Jewish man and raising a family learned that her entire life pivoted around one night. Once the eunuch in charge of the House of the Virgins decided it was her turn to visit the king's bedchamber, she would have to sleep with Xerxes whether she wanted to or not. If she did not provide him with a positive experience—memorable enough that he would ask for her by name—she would spend the rest of her life in the royal House of the Women, never to see the king again or rejoin her family.

Thousands of women like Hadassah and Angel have been viewed as commodities, not people. At this moment, women are being kidnapped as spoils of war and forcibly impregnated. Others are being held against their wills and sold into sex trafficking. Sex crimes are nothing new. They are driven by lust, an old evil that results in darkness and despair.

But this kind of evil does not have to result in *permanent* despair. Light can drive out darkness. Love can drive out hate. Esther found hope and light, and her story has been preserved in the Bible.

Likewise, young Sarah, abused and abandoned on that brothel bed, had not been forgotten by her Creator.

TO THINK ABOUT

1. Have you ever been made to feel like an object rather than a person? Did you do anything about it, or were you helpless in the situation? What were your feelings afterward, and how did you address them?

2. Were you familiar with the story of Hadassah/Esther before reading the summary? Had you heard that her situation was similar to a beauty pageant, or were you aware of the actual context? If you had been in Hadassah's situation, how would you have reacted to being forced to live in a king's harem? You can read Esther's complete story in the biblical book of Esther—it's a short book and well worth savoring.

3. Esther *did* sleep with the king, and he loved her so much he made her his queen. Later, when the king was conned into authorizing a decree that would give everyone in Persia the right to go out and murder Jews (*and* confiscate their property), Esther's cousin sent her a message: "Don't think for a moment that because you're in the palace you will escape when all other Jews are killed. If you keep quiet at a time like this, deliverance and relief for the Jews will arise from some other place, but you and your relatives will die. Who knows if perhaps you were made queen for just such a time as this?" (Esther 4:13–14). His message reminded Esther that God is always watching and always working . . . sometimes in ways we least expect.

God placed Esther in a strategic position to help her people. Where has God positioned you so you can have a positive impact on others? How might God want to use the trials of your past for a good purpose in your future as well as others'?

4. Recent years have brought a new awareness of sexual intimidation and abuse. Women are speaking out about situations ranging from social discomfort to rape, but what Angel and Esther endured could easily be considered worse than rape. They were captured for one purpose: to satisfy a man's pleasure. Esther was intended for an unstable, powerful king, and Angel for a succession of men who cared nothing about the little girl behind the pretty face. Why do you think women historically have been used and abused? Is it because we are usually physically weaker than most men? Or does our emotional makeup make us vulnerable?

5. God does not condone war between the sexes. We have already seen that God created Adam, then Eve. They were both given dominion over the earth. The wife is not inferior to the husband but equal to him before God. But in a marriage, because a two-headed creature will struggle to survive, the wife is to submit to the husband when they cannot agree (Ephesians 5:22). In all situations, public and private, we are to "be kindly affectionate to one another with brotherly love, in honor giving preference to one another" (Romans 12:10, NKJV).

God's bottom line is this: "There is no longer Jew or Gentile, slave or free, male and female. For you are all one in Christ Jesus" (Galatians 3:28).

Why do some women find it difficult to accept the idea that God wants men to lead in a marriage? (Lead—not demand. We're not talking about subjugation.) Why do some men think that husbandly leadership is husbandly lordship?

David got out of bed and was walking on the roof of the palace. As he looked out over the city, he noticed a woman of unusual beauty taking a bath. He sent someone to find out who she was, and he was told, "She is Bathsheba, the daughter of Eliam and the wife of Uriah the Hittite." Then David sent messengers to get her; and when she came to the palace, he slept with her. She had just completed the purification rites after having her menstrual period. Then she returned home. Later, when Bathsheba discovered that she was pregnant, she sent David a message, saying, "I'm pregnant." . . .

So the next morning David wrote a letter to Joab and gave it to Uriah to deliver. The letter instructed Joab, "Station Uriah on the front lines where the battle is fiercest. Then pull back so that he will be killed." So Joab assigned Uriah to a spot close to the city wall where he knew the enemy's strongest men were fighting. And when the enemy soldiers came out of the city to fight, Uriah the Hittite was killed along with several other Israelite soldiers. . . .

When Uriah's wife heard that her husband was dead, she mourned for him. When the period of mourning was over, David sent for her and brought her to the palace, and she became one of his wives. Then she gave birth to a son. But the LORD was displeased with what David had done. (2 Samuel 11:2–5, 14–17, 26–27)

Bathsheba was another beautiful woman seen, coveted, and taken by a powerful man, forced into a disaster engineered by someone else. She lost her husband and the child born to her and David. She knew long days of darkness and despair.

But God was not finished with Bathsheba, and later she gave birth to Solomon, arguably Israel's wisest and wealthiest king.

If you ever find yourself facing darkness and despair, know this: God is still watching and working. Your story is not finished.

Destruction

*Division is the same as creation; creation is
the same as destruction.*

CHUANG-TZU

A few years ago a friend of mine toured the Waterford Crystal factory in Waterford, Ireland. She loved watching the expert glassmakers work with the molten glass, blowing it and shaping it into amazingly graceful works of art. But Waterford Crystal is expensive, so most of the pieces were beyond her budget.

She jokingly asked her tour guide, "So, do you sell seconds in the store?"

He didn't laugh. "We would never put anything in the store that doesn't meet our standards," he said. "If a piece is flawed in any way, we melt it down and start over, turning it into something beautiful."

That image resonated with me. God is like a master artist, and He's an expert at taking a person who's been damaged by sin, refashioning her, and turning her into something amazing.

I suppose Chuang-tzu was right—sometimes destruction is the same process as creation. Though destruction brings pain, the result is worth the suffering.

PAIR-A-DICE LAY IN *the Mother Lode of California. It was the worst place Angel could have imagined, a shanty town of golden dreams built out of rotting sails from abandoned ships; a camp inhabited by outcasts and aristocrats, the displaced and dispossessed, the once-pampered and now-profane. Canvas-roofed bars and gambling houses lined mean streets ruled by unmasked depravity and greed, loneliness and grand illusions. Pair-a-Dice was wild jubilation. It wed black despair with fear and the foul taste of failure.*

Smiling cynically, Angel saw on one corner a man preaching salvation while on the other his brother, hat in hand, fleeced the godforsaken. Everywhere she looked, there were desperate men, exiled from home and family, seeking escape from the purgatory forged by their own decaying hopes for a future.

These same fools called her a Cyprian and sought solace where they were most assured of finding none—from her. They drew lots for her favors, four ounces of gold, payable in advance to the Duchess, madam of the Palace, the tent brothel where she lived. Any comer could have Angel for one half hour. Her own meager percentage would be kept under lock and key and guarded by a woman-hating giant named Magowan. As for the rest—those sad unfortunates who lacked the price to sample her talents—they stood knee-deep in a sea of mud called Main Street, waiting for a chance glimpse of "the Angel." And she lived a year in a month in this place that was unfit for anything but business. When would it end? How had all her desperate plans brought her here, to this horrible place of dirt and broken dreams?

When Angel appeared next in the story, the little girl had been completely destroyed. Sarah was gone, and nothing of her remained but buried memories. Prostitute Angel was cynical, sad, and weary, resigned to a life of mud and misery. She believed what Duke had taught her—that she was merely an object designed to give pleasure and was worthy of nothing more. Her beauty was still evident, but it brought her no joy, and the transitory pleasure it gave her customers was paid for with the men's blood, sweat, and tears.

Duke had destroyed Sarah and created a beautiful, callous creature with a heart as cold and unfeeling as the gold her customers stole out of the earth.

※

ANGEL HATED HER *life. She hated the Duchess. She hated Magowan. She hated her own wretched helplessness. Most of all she hated the men for their relentless quest for pleasure. She gave them her body but not a particle more. Maybe there wasn't any more. She didn't know. And that didn't seem to matter to any of the men. All they saw was her beauty, a flawless veil wrapped around a frozen heart, and they were enthralled. They looked into her angel eyes and were lost.*

She was not fooled by their endless declarations of love. They wanted her in the same way they wanted the gold in the streams. They lusted for her. They fought for the chance to be with her. They scrambled, grappled, gambled, and grabbed—and everything they had was spent without thought or consideration. They paid to become enslaved. She gave them what they thought was heaven and consigned them to hell.

What did it matter? She had nothing left. She didn't care. An even stronger force than the hatred that feasted on her was the weariness that sucked her soul dry. At eighteen, she was tired of living and resigned to the fact that nothing would ever change. She wondered why she had even been born. For this, she supposed. Take it or leave it. God's truth. And the only way to leave it was to kill herself. Every time she faced that fact, every time she had the chance, her courage failed.

Let's take a leap back in time to meet another woman, a real woman, who lived long before the Hebrews' exodus from Egypt.

Hagar was an Egyptian slave. We don't know how she came to be a slave. She might have been sold by impoverished parents who could not afford to feed her. She might have been snatched from her village by an enemy raiding party and sold at a market. She could have been sold into slavery as a young girl or teenager.

When the Bible introduces Hagar, she was a slave in Abram's household. By working hard and proving herself trustworthy, she earned the position of maidservant to seventy-five-year-old Sarai, the master's wife. Among the many slaves in Abram's possession, Hagar held a position of honor. Her duties included dressing Sarai, doing her hair, applying her cosmetics, running her errands, taking care of her clothing, drawing her baths—a long list of services, both personal and impersonal, all performed for Abram's wife.

We can assume the relationship between the two women was cordial, for what woman doesn't speak freely to her hairdresser? Hagar was no doubt attractive, for Sarai would have wanted an attendant that reflected well on her. As a woman without freedom of choice, Hagar might have been grateful she had not ended up in a worse place.

Sarai, however, faced a challenging situation: the Lord had promised Abram that he would be the father of a great nation (Genesis 12:2), but Abram had no sons. Once Sarai entered menopause and ceased to have a monthly menstrual cycle, she mourned, believing that some other woman would have the honor of bearing Abram's promised child.

But Sarai came up with a plan:

> Sarai said to Abram, "The LORD has prevented me from having children. Go and sleep with my servant. Perhaps I can have

children through her." And Abram agreed with Sarai's proposal. So Sarai, Abram's wife, took Hagar the Egyptian servant
and gave her to Abram as a wife. (16:2–3)

Hagar, a slave who had to obey or else face consequences ranging
from a whipping to being sold, knew of her mistress's struggle to
conceive. Perhaps she had offered suggestions about how to become
pregnant or consoled her mistress each time Sarai had missed another menstrual period, a sure sign that she remained barren. As
Sarai's personal handmaiden, Hagar had to be well acquainted with
the intimate details of Sarai's life.

One day, maybe while Hagar was braiding Sarai's hair, the mistress suggested the unthinkable: "You have served me well for many
years, Hagar. Now I want you to serve me in another way. Sleep
with my husband until you become pregnant. Then, because you
are mine, the child you conceive will be mine as well."

Hagar must have stuttered in disbelief. Sleep with the master? A
handmaiden who seduced her master of her own volition could be
killed. Yet here was Sarai suggesting something that ought not to be
done. Hadn't Abram often told his servants that God wanted men
to leave their parents and unite with their wives so they would be
one? Furthermore, Abram was old, in his mideighties!

As much as she may have despised the idea, Hagar had to obey.
For the next several nights, she left her mistress and went into the
master's tent.

Abram had sexual relations with Hagar, and she became pregnant. But when Hagar knew she was pregnant, she began to
treat her mistress, Sarai, with contempt. Then Sarai said to
Abram, "This is all your fault! I put my servant into your arms,
but now that she's pregnant she treats me with contempt. The
LORD will show who's wrong—you or me!"

Abram replied, "Look, she is your servant, so deal with her

as you see fit." Then Sarai treated Hagar so harshly that she finally ran away. (verses 4–6)

When Hagar became pregnant, her attitude changed. Her preg-
nancy dismissed a theory that may have given Sarai a glimmer of
comfort—that maybe the problem was Abram's. Maybe he was ster-
ile, not her . . .

But now everyone knew Abram's lack of an heir was Sarai's fault.
He was fertile! In that area, at least, Hagar was of more value than
her mistress. Along with her burgeoning belly, which Sarai couldn't
help but see every day, Hagar demonstrated a superior attitude, and
Sarai could not tolerate it. But what could she do? She didn't dare
whip the slave for fear of harming the unborn child.

Maybe Sarai lay awake at night, nursing her jealousy and imag-
ining ways she could punish Hagar without doing physical damage.
We do know she made her handmaiden's life so miserable that the
pregnant slave ran away.

> The angel of the LORD found Hagar beside a spring of water in
> the wilderness, along the road to Shur. The angel said to her,
> "Hagar, Sarai's servant, where have you come from, and where
> are you going?"
>
> "I'm running away from my mistress, Sarai," she replied.
>
> The angel of the LORD said to her, "Return to your mis-
> tress, and submit to her authority." Then he added, "I will give
> you more descendants than you can count."
>
> And the angel also said, "You are now pregnant and will
> give birth to a son. You are to name him Ishmael (which
> means 'God hears'), for the LORD has heard your cry of dis-
> tress. This son of yours will be a wild man, as untamed as a
> wild donkey! He will raise his fist against everyone, and every-
> one will be against him. Yes, he will live in open hostility
> against all his relatives."

Thereafter, Hagar used another name to refer to the LORD, who had spoken to her. She said, "You are the God who sees me." She also said, "Have I truly seen the One who sees me?" So that well was named Beer-lahai-roi (which means "well of the Living One who sees me"). It can still be found between Kadesh and Bered.

So Hagar gave Abram a son, and Abram named him Ishmael. Abram was eighty-six years old when Ishmael was born. (verses 7–16)

TO THINK ABOUT

1. Many people question their faith when bad things happen to innocent people. Some even say they can't believe in the goodness of God when such things occur. After all, Sarah did nothing to deserve ending up in the clutches of people like Duke and the Duchess. However, sometimes we must struggle through the rough times of the present in order to appreciate what God will do in the future.

Joseph's brothers sold him into slavery, but God lifted him out of bondage in Egypt, elevating him to the position of Pharaoh's right-hand man, where he was responsible for saving thousands of lives during a severe seven-year famine. (Read the entire fascinating story in Genesis 37, 39–47.) How do perspective and time change our views of tragic situations?

2. In a real sense, Hagar was a victim of sex trafficking. She was sold, compelled to sleep with an old man, and forced to bear his child, who was then taken from her. She ran for her life, came close to dying in the desert, and was well acquainted with bleak despair. What parallels do you see between Hagar and Angel? In what ways are they alike? How do they—or their responses—differ?

3. Think of the lowest point in your life. Now that you've pinned it down, did you arrive at that wretched time because of your own actions, or were you in an emotional valley because of the actions of others? How did God work in your life during that time, and how did He bring you up from that low point?

James reminds us, "Consider it all joy, my brethren, when you encounter various trials, knowing that the testing of your faith produces endurance. And let endurance have its perfect result, so that you may be perfect and complete, lacking in nothing" (James 1:2–4, NASB). Life is like boot camp. We learn to obey our Commander. We undergo testing and trials in order to grow stronger and more mature.

4. Angel thought her life was worthless, but God was not finished with her. He was about to send a man to love her, cherish her, and redeem her from slavery. She did not even know God, and what she recalled of Him from her mother's life had only made her bitter and cynical.

But God had not forgotten her. He did not forget Hagar but heard her cries and comforted her. After meeting God in the desert, Hagar demonstrated faith in His promise and obeyed His command. How did she demonstrate faith? How did she obey?

God told Israel, "Yes, I have loved you with an everlasting love; therefore with lovingkindness I have drawn you" (Jeremiah 31:3, NKJV). That is how He drew Hagar and Angel. It's how He will draw you.

In what ways have you experienced the loving-kindness of God?

Bless the LORD, O my soul;
And all that is within me, bless His holy name!
Bless the LORD, O my soul,
And forget not all His benefits:
Who forgives all your iniquities,
Who heals all your diseases,
Who redeems your life from destruction,
Who crowns you with lovingkindness and tender mercies,
Who satisfies your mouth with good things,
So that your youth is renewed like the eagle's.
   (Psalm 103:1–5, NKJV)

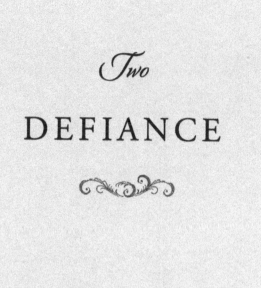

Two

DEFIANCE

I'VE BEEN DEFIANT OVER the years, though I may not have thought of my behavior that way in the moment. Most of us tend to think of defiance as marching in protest against something or someone, carrying placards, and shouting slogans or names at those who believe differently than we do. We presume we are in the right and the other side is wrong. We might even call those who stand against us "evil." We raise our fists and see defiance as our human right.

Maybe our defiance doesn't show in open rebellion but does in the way we think and how we view ourselves. We're born defiant. We see it in a child who stamps a foot: *I want what I want and I want it now* and *I don't want to obey.*

Defiance comes in many forms, some so subtle that no one, even the defiant one, would recognize it. Willfulness shows up when we think, *It's my life and I'll do as I please.* It's easy to fall into step with that philosophy in a culture permeated by the belief that people can decide what is right for themselves.

My defiance showed up whenever I smothered my conscience and did as I pleased. I defied God by doing whatever I thought was right at the moment, even when I knew at gut level that I was doing wrong. We can so easily justify and rationalize our behavior, convincing ourselves that wrong is right and right is wrong. Even now, after years of walking with Jesus, I catch myself going down that dead-end road. And I have to choose. Will I rebel? Or will I trust God to know what's best for me?

Adam rebelled when he reached out, took the forbidden fruit Eve offered him, and ate it. It wasn't just a matter of wanting to be like God. Adam wanted to be the god of his own life. As Adam's descendants, we think we know ourselves so well we can decide what is best for us.

Angel blamed God for everything that had happened to her mother and to her. Hadn't He abandoned them the same way Alex Stafford had? In Angel's mind, God was like Duke, a powerful, cruel despot who punished her severely whenever she fought him. No hope was to be found in Him.

The truth is this: the only source of hope and everlasting, unfailing love is God revealed through Christ Jesus. Just as Michael wooed Angel to that knowledge, the loving-kindness of Christian neighbors and friends wooed me. I saw their faith in action. As they came alongside me, pointing the way, I stopped rebelling against God and opened my heart, inviting Him in.

I'm still human. I still have that nature to rebel against God, to want my own way. When that temptation comes, I sense a gentle voice reminding me of the pain I bring on myself by defying His wisdom. God is God, and I am not. Will I trust Him, or will I insist on my own way?

It's a question each of us must answer.

Master of Her Fate

It matters not how strait the gate,
How charged with punishments the scroll,
I am the master of my fate:
I am the captain of my soul.

WILLIAM ERNEST HENLEY, "INVICTUS"

ANGEL'S FOOT STOPPED *and she leaned forward. "What about you, mister? What's your name? You from any place in particular? Do you have a wife somewhere? Are you afraid to do what you really want?"*

She was leveling all barrels at him, but rather than be taken aback, he felt himself relaxing. This girl was more real to him than the one who had greeted him at the door. "Michael Hosea," he said. "I live in a valley southwest of here, and I'm not married, but I will be soon."

She frowned uneasily. It was the way he was looking at her. The intensity unnerved her. "What sort of name is Hosea?"

His smile became wry. "Prophetic."

Was he making a joke at her expense? "Are you going to tell me my future?"

"You're going to marry me, and I'm going to take you out of here."

She laughed. "Well, my third proposal today. I'm so flattered." Shaking her head, she leaned forward again, her smile cold and cynical. Did he think this was a new approach? Did he think it was neces-sary? "When would you like me to start playing my part, mister?"

"*After the ring's on your finger. Right now, I want to get to know you a little better.*"

She hated him for dragging the game on. The wasted time, the hypocrisy, the endless lies. It had been a long night, and she was in no mood to humor him. "*What's to tell? What I do is what I am. All it comes down to is you telling me how you want me to be. But be quick. Your time's almost up.*"

Michael saw he had made a fine mess of this first meeting. What had he expected? To come in here, talk plain, and walk out with her on his arm? She looked like she wanted to give him the boot. He was angry at himself for being such a naive fool. "*You're not talking love, Mara, and I didn't come here to use you.*"

The steady deepness of his words and that name—Mara—roused her anger even more. "*No?*" She tilted her chin. "*Well, I think I understand.*" She stood. He was sitting and she moved close, her soft hands combing into his hair. She could feel his tension and relished it.

"*Let me guess, mister. You want to get to know me. You want to find out how I think and what I feel. And most of all, you want to know how a nice girl like me got into a business like this.*"

"*You're telling me this is the life you want?*"

What did want have to do with anything? "*This is my life.*"

"*It doesn't have to be. If you had a choice, what would you want?*"

"*From you? Nothing.*"

"*From living.*"

A bleakness settled inside her. Living? What was he talking about? She felt battered by his questions and defended herself with an aloof, cool smile. Spreading her hands, she showed off her simple room with its spare furnishings. "*I have everything I need right here.*"

"*You've got a roof, food, and fine clothes.*"

"*And work,*" she said tightly. "*Oh, don't you forget my work. I'm real good at it.*"

"*You hate it.*"

She was silent a moment, wary. "You just drew me on one of my bad nights." She went to the window. Pretending to look out, she closed her eyes and fought for control. What was wrong with her this evening? What was it about this man that got to her? She preferred the numbness to this stirring of emotion. Hope was torment; hope was an enemy. And this man was a thorn in her side.

When Michael Hosea spoke to Angel for the first time, he asked her to marry him, and he meant it. He fully intended to love her, care for her, provide for her, and take her away from the life of slavery that she hated, but she denied his proposal. She refused to believe his offer was sincere.

Angel was like many men and women today. They are miserable, but they are in control of their lives—at least they think so. They are like the character in the poem "Invictus," full of bravado as he says he doesn't care whether he makes it through the "strait . . . gate" (the gate of heaven) or how many sins he has racked up in God's book when he dies—at least he is the master of his fate and the captain of his soul.[2]

And he's right, but he's the captain of a doomed ship. Perhaps it would be better to hand his ship over to a master sailor.

Earlier I mentioned Adam's willingness to ignore God's command and eat the forbidden fruit. We all inherited that willfulness, which shows up at an early age. Babies not even a year old can exhibit anger if you take toys from them or if they aren't fed the instant they decide they're hungry. Babies are self-centered because they are the suns of their small universes and everything revolves around them.

Some people never outgrow that "I'm the center of the universe" mindset.

One young man approached Jesus to ask a question:

"Teacher, what good deed must I do to have eternal life?"

"Why ask me about what is good?" Jesus replied. "There is only One who is good. But to answer your question—if you want to receive eternal life, keep the commandments."

"Which ones?" the man asked.

And Jesus replied: "'You must not murder. You must not commit adultery. You must not steal. You must not testify falsely. Honor your father and mother. Love your neighbor as yourself.'"

"I've obeyed all these commandments," the young man replied. "What else must I do?"

Jesus told him, "If you want to be perfect, go and sell all your possessions and give the money to the poor, and you will have treasure in heaven. Then come, follow me."

But when the young man heard this, he went away sad, for he had many possessions. (Matthew 19:16–22)

The wealthy young man was fine with following Jesus as long as *he* controlled the situation. He was happy to be moral, honor his parents, and love his neighbor (in words, at least). But then Jesus added one more task, one that came with a price tag: "If you want to be the sort of man who enters heaven, give away everything you have and follow Me."

The young man couldn't commit to that—not only because he loved his creature comforts but also because he would be submitting control of his entire life, including his possessions, to Jesus. And that he could not do.

I've often heard people say that salvation is a free gift, and it is. Jesus paid the price for our sin, and all we have to do is accept His gift. But accepting that gift requires surrendering our sin and our lives to Jesus, exchanging our old lives for the new ones He wants to give us, in which He is our master and we are His servants. Not everyone wants that deal.

We live in an increasingly secular society, one in which the Judeo-Christian values of generations past have been turned on their heads. "Love your neighbor" changed to "Tolerate your neighbor" and then to "*Approve of* your neighbor," even when your neighbor does things God condemns. Society tells us we have the right to abort our babies, have sex with whomever we want, partake freely of mind-altering substances, and otherwise live however we choose while never *ever* pointing out that God condemns such activities.

How will the world know that God set standards for human behavior unless we tell them? God's Word says that we should not murder and that we are to exercise control over our appetites, have sex with only our spouses, respect our bodies as the temple of the Holy Spirit, and bear witness to the truth. We do not expect people of other faiths or even people of no faith to live as we do, but when we submit ourselves to Christ, we stop being defiant in mind and voice. We can't give our lives to Jesus with an exception clause: "I'll obey in this area but not that one."

Angel was more than willing to have sex with Michael Hosea, but he wasn't seeking a shallow physical encounter. He wanted *all* of her and knew he'd have to win her trust before he could win her heart. Having sex is not the way to win someone's heart.

Angel was openly defiant—she flaunted her cynicism and mocked and scorned Michael, even while his persistence got under her skin. He was different, and oh, how she needed something different.

But in order to gain it, she would have to stop resisting, and she'd been defiant for too long to stop after one brief meeting.

TO THINK ABOUT

1. What does it mean to call yourself a Christian? Is it a label you can put on and take off? What does being a Christian mean to *you*? Does your belief align with what you read about in today's lesson?

2. Our society celebrates humanism, a philosophy that focuses on human goodness, human efforts, and human needs. God plays no role in humanism because the humanist sees people as the top of the evolutionary pyramid. Songs like "Greatest Love of All" by Whitney Houston may have lovely tunes, but the lyrics are purely humanistic. Loving yourself isn't the greatest love; God's redemptive love for fallen, sinful humanity is the greatest love men and women will ever know.

What are some other examples of humanism replacing the societal belief that God rules over the affairs of people? How do you see this exhibited in movies, music, commercials, and books?

3. We tend to celebrate heroes who defy unjust laws, practices, or verdicts. But defiance in itself is neutral—neither positive nor negative. Someone who defies *just* laws, practices, or verdicts may be exercising free speech, but that sort of defiance is foolish.

How did you feel when Angel defied Michael Hosea? When she defied the Duchess? Magowan? Was her defiance always wise?

4. Have you ever openly defied anyone? As a teenager, did you defy your parents? How did that turn out?

5. Defiance is fueled by anger. What was the source of Angel's anger? What was the source of yours when you have been rebellious?

Defiance is open refusal to obey authority. Defiance is evil when the authority is legitimate but good when the authority is ungodly.

No one should defy God.

> *Send out a call for archers to come to Babylon.*
> *Surround the city so none can escape.*
> *Do to her as she has done to others,*
> *for she has defied the LORD, the Holy One of Israel.*
> *(Jeremiah 50:29)*

To defy God's people is to defy God.

> *David replied to the Philistine, "You come to me with sword,*
> *spear, and javelin, but I come to you in the name of the LORD*
> *of Heaven's Armies—the God of the armies of Israel, whom*
> *you have defied. Today the LORD will conquer you, and I will*
> *kill you and cut off your head. And then I will give the dead*
> *bodies of your men to the birds and wild animals, and the*
> *whole world will know that there is a God in Israel! And ev-*
> *eryone assembled here will know that the LORD rescues his*
> *people, but not with sword and spear. This is the LORD's bat-*
> *tle, and he will give you to us!" (1 Samuel 17:45–47)*

Defiance of legitimate authority is evil.

> *Everyone must submit to governing authorities. For all au-*
> *thority comes from God, and those in positions of authority*
> *have been placed there by God. So anyone who rebels against*
> *authority is rebelling against what God has instituted, and*
> *they will be punished. (Romans 13:1–2)*

For the Lord's sake, submit to all human authority—whether the king as head of state, or the officials he has appointed. For the king has sent them to punish those who do wrong and to honor those who do right.

It is God's will that your honorable lives should silence those ignorant people who make foolish accusations against you. For you are free, yet you are God's slaves, so don't use your freedom as an excuse to do evil. Respect everyone, and love the family of believers. Fear God, and respect the king. (1 Peter 2:13–17)

Defiance of ungodly authority is praiseworthy.

Nebuchadnezzar said, "Praise to the God of Shadrach, Meshach, and Abednego! He sent his angel to rescue his servants who trusted in him. They defied the king's command and were willing to die rather than serve or worship any god except their own God." (Daniel 3:28)

"We gave you strict orders never again to teach in this man's name!" he said. "Instead, you have filled all Jerusalem with your teaching about him, and you want to make us responsible for his death!"

But Peter and the apostles replied, "We must obey God rather than any human authority." (Acts 5:28–29)

Defiant Heart

*A heart can no more be forced to love than a stomach can
be forced to digest food by persuasion.*

ALFRED NOBEL

MICHAEL CAME BACK *in with an armload of firewood.*

"Mister, I don't know the first thing about what a farm wife does."

He stacked the wood neatly. "I didn't expect you would."

"Then just what chores did you have in mind?"

"Cooking, washing, ironing, the garden."

"I just told you—"

*"You're smart. You'll learn." He put another log on the fire. "You
won't be doing anything really heavy until you're able, which you won't
be for another month at least."*

*Really heavy? What did that mean? She decided to take another
tack instead. Her mouth curved in a well-practiced smile. "What
about the other wifely duties?"*

*Michael glanced back at her. "When it means something more to
you than work, we'll consummate the marriage."*

*She was taken aback by his frankness. Where was the farmer who
blushed and jumped when she touched him? Unnerved, she retreated*

in anger. "Fine, mister. I'll do whatever you've got in mind. I'll match
you hour for hour, day for day since you started taking care of me."

"And when you figure we're square, you'll leave. Is that it?"

"I'm going back to Pair-a-Dice and get what the Duchess owes
me."

"No, you're not," he said quietly.

"Yes, I am." She would get her money from the Duchess even if she
had to take it out of the old crone's hide. Then she would hire someone
to build her a cabin just like this one, far enough away from a town so
she wouldn't hear the noise and smell the stench, but close enough that
she could get what supplies she needed. She would buy a gun, a big
gun, and plenty of bullets, and if any man came around knocking at
her door, she would use it, unless she needed some money. Then she
would have to let him in to do business first. But if she was careful and
smart, she could live a long time on what she had already earned. She
could hardly wait. She had never lived all by herself, and it would be
heaven.

You were left to yourself for an entire week, *a small voice mocked*
her from deep inside, and you were miserable, remember? Admit it,
being by yourself isn't heaven at all. Not when you have so many
demons to keep you company.

"You may have paid a lot of gold dust for me, but you don't own
me, mister."

Michael studied her with patience. She was small and weak but
possessed an iron will. It shone from her defiant blue eyes and the rigid
way she was holding herself. She thought she had enough to overcome
him. She was wrong. He was doing God's will, and he had plans of his
own, plans that kept growing, but he had said all he was going to say
for a while. Let her think on it.

"You're right," he said. "I don't own you, but you're not running
away from this."

Angel set the plate on the side table. She was shaking violently but
was still determined not to lie down. She studied him. Sooner or later,

she would figure him out. He was a man, wasn't he? He couldn't be that complex. She would take him apart piece by piece.

Angel had known all about Duke after the first night. He liked power. He wanted immediate obedience. She didn't have to like what he wanted to do, as long as she did it. With a smile. Hesitance earned that cold, dark look; protest, a slap; defiance, brute force. Running away earned the end of his lit cheroot. By the time he tired of keeping her all to himself, she had learned one major lesson: to pretend. No matter what she felt, no matter how frightened or repulsed or angry, pretend to like whatever the men wanted and paid to get. And if she couldn't pretend to like it, she had to pretend not to care. She had become real good at that.

Thanks to abusive treatment by Duke and others, Angel built a strong wall around her heart. Her real feelings, her deep emotions, were hidden behind a wall of scars. She learned to mask her emotions while pretending to be charming, sexy, and adventurous. When that approach didn't work on Michael, she adopted a tough, callous attitude.

After a person is wounded, erecting a wall around his or her emotions is a logical and common form of self-defense. Even neglected babies instinctively do it. Rather than risking emotional attachment, infants who do not have consistent caregivers will refuse to meet the eyes of anyone who feeds them their bottles.

The heart, which pumps oxygen-rich blood throughout our bodies, is said to be the seat of our emotions, but our emotional center really lies in the brain. Our emotional attachments and resources are rooted in the temporal lobe, specifically in the amygdala, the headquarters for processing feelings. But it's not very romantic to say, "I love you with all my amygdala," is it?

For simplicity's sake, let's consider the heart the seat of human passion. The thing about our emotions is that they are not infallible. They are fickle, burning hot and then growing cold. They can be inflamed by lies. The Bible recognizes this and cautions, "The human heart is the most deceitful of all things, and desperately wicked. Who really knows how bad it is?" (Jeremiah 17:9).

When I was a child, I went home to an empty house, both parents still at work. Living in the country, I had no friends nearby, so I created imaginary friends and carried on audible conversations as I made myself a snack, played, or did my homework. That habit was broken when my older brother and his Boy Scout friends hid in the house, planning to jump out and scare me. One boy said he stayed hidden because he thought someone else was in the house with me. Nope. Just me and my voices. I didn't carry on audible conversations after that, but scenes and conversations continued to play out in my head. Confession: they still do. That's why I became a writer.

During my time as a young bride, these silent but lively imaginary conversations continued. If Rick looked upset, I assumed it had something to do with me. My mind whirred with defense or apology or angry monologues. I'd imagine what Rick might say. Sometimes I'd be sure he had said something, and he would deny it, and I'd insist, until I realized it had come from some member of the chorus in my own head. Our minds are always active, aren't they? Sometimes we relive past experiences, good and bad. Sometimes we edit them. We dream and sometimes awaken shaking from the seeming reality of what we were experiencing in our imaginations.

When I started writing, Rick would come home from work and ask, "Am I the good guy today or the bad guy?"

Why? Because I had trouble stepping out of my make-believe world into the real one. Eventually I learned how to shut down my imagination, turn off the story playing inside my head, and reenter the real world I live in with my husband. And after decades of being married to me, Rick knows when my mind is in another era, carrying on conversations with characters who become real to me even though I know they don't actually live and breathe. And I've learned that when Rick is upset, it seldom has to do with something I have or haven't done. It could be his favorite baseball team just traded another beloved player. We've both learned to just ask, "Do you want to talk about it?" And we do talk about what's happening in our lives, things that trouble us, and our hopes and dreams and fears.

Women as deeply wounded as Angel tend to invent lies to help themselves survive. Angel's past convinced her that she was not worth anything. That God did not love her or have any plan to help her. That the only way she would ever be happy was if she could live as a recluse somewhere, without any men or other women around.

Her raw emotions persuaded her that those beliefs were true, but they weren't. She was worth a great deal, and Michael Hosea knew it. God did love her and had already set in motion a plan for her restoration, but she couldn't see it. And she would never have been happy as a recluse, as her week alone in the house had already demonstrated.

But her heart was still defiant, her emotions still fixated on false beliefs. But you know the good thing about emotions? They can change.

TO THINK ABOUT

Each of the following Bible passages tells us something about human emotions. Read each passage, and note what it teaches.

1. Emotions can lead us to sin.

> Later [Eve] gave birth to [Cain's] brother and named him Abel.
> When they grew up, Abel became a shepherd, while Cain cultivated the ground. When it was time for the harvest, Cain

presented some of his crops as a gift to the LORD. Abel also brought a gift—the best portions of the firstborn lambs from his flock. The LORD accepted Abel and his gift, but he did not accept Cain and his gift. This made Cain very angry, and he looked dejected.

"Why are you so angry?" the LORD asked Cain. "Why do you look so dejected? You will be accepted if you do what is right. But if you refuse to do what is right, then watch out! Sin is crouching at the door, eager to control you. But you must subdue it and be its master."

One day Cain suggested to his brother, "Let's go out into the fields." And while they were in the field, Cain attacked his brother, Abel, and killed him. (Genesis 4:2–8)

Have your emotions ever led you to do something sinful? How did you handle the situation afterward?

2. Emotions can lead us to make foolish decisions.

The Spirit of the LORD came upon Jephthah, and he went throughout the land of Gilead and Manasseh, including Mizpah in Gilead, and from there he led an army against the Ammonites. And Jephthah made a vow to the LORD. He said, "If you give me victory over the Ammonites, I will give to the LORD whatever comes out of my house to meet me when I return in triumph. I will sacrifice it as a burnt offering."

So Jephthah led his army against the Ammonites, and the LORD gave him victory. . . .

When Jephthah returned home to Mizpah, his daughter came out to meet him, playing on a tambourine and dancing for joy. She was his one and only child; he had no other sons or daughters. When he saw her, he tore his clothes in anguish. "Oh, my daughter!" he cried out. "You have completely destroyed me! You've brought disaster on me! For I have made a vow to the LORD, and I cannot take it back."

And she said, "Father, if you have made a vow to the LORD, you must do to me what you have vowed, for the LORD has given you a great victory over your enemies, the Ammonites. But first let me do this one thing: Let me go up and roam in the hills and weep with my friends for two months, because I will die a virgin."

"You may go," Jephthah said. And he sent her away for two months. She and her friends went into the hills and wept because she would never have children. When she returned home, her father kept the vow he had made, and she died a virgin. (Judges 11:29–32, 34–39)

Have emotions ever led you to make a rash decision? Were you able to correct your mistake?

3. God understands our emotions and heals those with broken hearts.

The LORD is close to the brokenhearted;

he rescues those whose spirits are crushed. (Psalm 34:18)

When you've been brokenhearted and grieving, have you ever felt the comfort of the Holy Spirit? How did the Spirit comfort you?

4. We must guard our emotions because they can destroy us.

Guard your heart above all else,

for it determines the course of your life. (Proverbs 4:23)

Enthusiasm without knowledge is no good;

haste makes mistakes. (19:2)

Have your emotions ever led you to make an impulsive decision you regretted? To make a bad decision that changed the course of your life?

5. Jesus experiences emotions, and so do God the Father and the Holy Spirit.

> When Jesus saw [Mary] weeping and saw the other people
> wailing with her, a deep anger welled up within him, and he
> was deeply troubled. "Where have you put him?" he asked
> them.
>   They told him, "Lord, come and see." Then Jesus wept.
> (John 11:33–35)

Why do you think Jesus wept? Out of sorrow for Lazarus's death or out of frustration because the mourners did not believe He could resurrect His friend?

6. Our actions and emotions can grieve the Holy Spirit. Or we can set aside some emotions in favor of others. We do not have to be slaves to bitterness, anger, and fear.

> Do not bring sorrow to God's Holy Spirit by the way you live.
> Remember, he has identified you as his own, guaranteeing that
> you will be saved on the day of redemption.
>   Get rid of all bitterness, rage, anger, harsh words, and slan-
> der, as well as all types of evil behavior. Instead, be kind to
> each other, tenderhearted, forgiving one another, just as God
> through Christ has forgiven you. (Ephesians 4:30–32)

When was a time you grieved the Holy Spirit and felt His conviction? When have you wanted to react in anger but chose to respond with understanding?

Oswald Chambers tells us that apart from the Spirit of God, men and women have no emotion toward God; they are spiritually dead.[3] But when the Holy Spirit gives life to us through the Word of God, that life affects our emotions.

Before Angel met Michael, she certainly had no emotional response to God other than anger. But when the Spirit began to move in her heart, her emotions awoke in new and unsettling ways. Unpleasant emotions ensured she would experience growing pains.

But tension can be a sign of new life, the beginning of a new existence.

At Arm's Length

Touch seems to be as essential as sunlight.
DIANE ACKERMAN, *A NATURAL HISTORY OF THE SENSES*

MICHAEL HOSEA WAS *unloading crates of vegetables from the back of his buckboard when he saw a beautiful young woman walking along the street. She was dressed in black, like a widow, and a big, rough-looking man with a gun on his hip was at her side. All along Main Street, men stopped what they were doing, took off their hats, and watched her. She said not a word to anyone. She looked neither to the right nor the left. She moved with simple, fluid grace, her shoulders straight, her head held high.*

Michael couldn't take his eyes off her. His heart beat faster and faster as she came near. He willed her to look at him, but she didn't. He let out his breath after she passed him, not even aware that he had been holding it.

This one, beloved.

Michael felt a rush of adrenaline mingled with joy. Lord. Lord!

"Something, ain't she?" Joseph Hochschild said.

Michael shouldered a barrel of apples. "What do you know about her?"

"No more than anyone else, I guess. She takes long walks. It's a habit of hers. Does it every Monday, Wednesday, and Friday afternoon about this same time." He nodded toward the men along the street. *"They all come to watch her."*

"Who's the man with her?" A dismal thought occurred to him. *"Her husband?"*

"Husband?" He laughed. *"More like a bodyguard. His name's Magowan. He makes certain nobody bothers her. No one gets within a foot of her unless they've paid their dues."*

Michael frowned slightly and went back outside. He stood at the back of his wagon, staring after her. She caught at something deep inside him. There was a grave, tragic dignity about her. As the storekeeper hefted another crate, Michael asked the question burning inside him. *"How do I meet her, Joseph?"*

❦

WHEN MICHAEL TURNED, *his wife stood naked before the fire, waiting for him. She was breathtaking, just as Eve must have been. Michael came to her in wonder.*

Oh, Lord, she is so perfect, like no other creation in the world. My mate. *He swung her up into his arms and kissed her.*

As he stretched out beside her on their marriage bed, he marveled at how she fit him, flesh to flesh, molded for him. "Oh, Jesus," *he whispered, awestruck by the gift.*

Angel felt him shaking violently and knew it was due to his long, self-imposed celibacy. Strangely, she was not repulsed. Instead, she felt an alien sense of sympathy. She pushed the feelings away, blocking him out of her mind—and was surprised when he drew back from her and searched her eyes, his own filled with so much she turned her face away.

Think of your money in Pair-a-Dice, Angel. Think of going back and getting it from the Duchess. Think of having some-

thing for yourself. **Think of being free. Don't think about this man.** *It had worked for her in the past. Why not now?* **Come on, Angel. Remember how you used to close your mind? You've done it before. Do it again. Don't think. Don't feel. Just play the part. He'll never know.**

But Michael wasn't like other men, and he did know. He didn't have to die to realize she had brought him to the edge of heaven and slammed the gates in his face.

"Beloved," he said, turning her face back to him. "Why won't you let me get close to you?"

≈ ⚬⚭⚬ ≈

When *Redeeming Love* began, Angel's authentic self was locked away in her mind. Her figure was beautiful and appealing to men, but although Angel may have shared her body with them, she did not share anything of her true self. Everything she gave the men who visited her in Pair-a-Dice was false—from her smile to her physical responses.

By the time Michael Hosea entered her life, Angel was so locked inside her mind that she could not be free with him. In their early days together, all she could give him was the false Angel—and though she offered him her body and her skills, he didn't want the false self. He wanted to know the woman beneath the emotional scars, but Angel would not even give him her true name.

> *"I'm not saying I'm any better than any other man who comes to you. I just want more."*
>
> *"Such as?"*
>
> *"Everything. I want what you don't even know you have to give."*
>
> *"Some men expect a whole lot for a couple of ounces of gold dust."*

The Bible tells us the story of another woman who was locked away for years—twelve, to be exact:

A man named Jairus, a leader of the local synagogue, came and fell at Jesus' feet, pleading with him to come home with him. His only daughter, who was about twelve years old, was dying.

As Jesus went with him, he was surrounded by the crowds. A woman in the crowd had suffered for twelve years with constant bleeding, and she could find no cure. Coming up behind Jesus, she touched the fringe of his robe. Immediately, the bleeding stopped.

"Who touched me?" Jesus asked.

Everyone denied it, and Peter said, "Master, this whole crowd is pressing up against you."

But Jesus said, "Someone deliberately touched me, for I felt healing power go out from me." When the woman realized that she could not stay hidden, she began to tremble and fell to her knees in front of him. The whole crowd heard her explain why she had touched him and that she had been immediately healed. "Daughter," he said to her, "your faith has made you well. Go in peace." (Luke 8:41–48)

This woman—the Bible does not give us her name—was probably bleeding from the uterus. It could have been a wound of another sort, but since the Bible does not specifically name her illness, we can assume it was bleeding from the female organs.

Having a twelve-year menstrual period was more than an inconvenient problem in biblical Israel. Normal menstruation produced uncleanness that lasted for seven days from the first day of bleeding. While a woman was unclean, she could not go to the temple or visit friends. Everything she sat on or touched was considered unclean and had to be purified. If a person touched her bed, that person had to wash his or her clothes and bathe in water and remain unclean until evening. If a woman had bleeding unrelated to her menstrual period, she was unclean for as long as the discharge continued (Leviticus 15:19–28).

Can you imagine living with someone—or even being a friend of someone—you could not touch for fear of becoming unclean? The woman who quietly followed Jesus through the crowd was desperate for healing. She had been to every doctor in the area and had spent all her money trying to find a cure (Mark 5:26). Plus, she had prayed. For weeks, months, and years, she had begged God to take away the mysterious bleeding that had ruined her life.

As Angel had, this woman withdrew into herself. She did not dare make friends, for how could she be warm and hospitable when no one could visit or touch her without becoming unclean? She probably had a husband in her youth, but what man would want to remain married to a woman he could not touch? He could not sit where she sat; he could not eat food she had prepared. If he did, her uncleanness passed to him, which meant he could not go to the temple or synagogue or participate in the religious life of the community until he became ritually clean again. I imagine her husband eventually left her because he could see no reason why her illness should destroy his life.

Then this woman heard about Jesus and His power to heal. Lurking behind corners, careful not to be seen or to touch anyone or to sit on a bench, she overheard stories about Him feeding the hungry, making the lame walk, and restoring sight to the blind. Rumors were He *touched* people, even sick people—He held their hands, wiped their faces, and placed His hands on their heads—and she could never allow Him to touch her. Though her condition was not visible, everyone in town knew she was unclean, as untouchable as a leper.

So she walked toward the crowd that had gathered to greet the man from Nazareth. She lingered in the shadows, her veil drawn over her face, as Jairus, a leader in the synagogue, asked the young rabbi to come see his sick daughter.

And as Jesus followed Jairus, the bleeding woman threaded her way through the throng, moving like a shadow, careful not to touch anyone but the One who mattered. She bent and reached out—there! Her fingertips brushed the fringe at the edge of His prayer shawl.

He stopped and turned, His gaze sweeping the crowd. "Who touched Me?"

Her heart pounded heavily, but more than that, the dull ache that lived inside her faded. The warm stickiness between her legs stopped flowing, and she knew a single touch had brought healing.

All around, heads turned, eyes wide, brows lifting in silent question. "How can You ask that?" one of His disciples asked. "You are in the middle of a crowd; *everyone* is touching You."

Jesus shook His head and smiled. "Someone deliberately touched Me. I felt healing power go out of Me."

Then she felt the pressure of His eyes on her. Would He back away in revulsion? Would He throw His now unclean prayer shawl to the ground? Would He chide her for venturing out in public?

Trembling, she lifted her head and met the Teacher's gaze, then crumpled to her knees. "I did, Lord. I touched You."

He did not recoil in distaste. He looked at her with eyes filled with understanding, and He nodded. "Daughter, your faith has made you well. Go in peace."

TO THINK ABOUT

1. Babies who are not held or cuddled often fail to thrive. God designed our bodies to bond through touch, even when we are older. When is the last time you touched someone outside your family? When was the last time you were touched? Was it a positive experience? If not, why not?

2. While working in Pair-a-Dice, Angel was touched but in an impersonal manner; men used physical intimacy to exploit her body to satisfy their own desires but never hers. Why did Michael Hosea's touch affect her differently? What would have been her reaction if he had been with her as a husband right away?

3. None of us wants to be manhandled or have our personal space violated by a stranger, but sometimes a human touch can make all the difference to a person's perspective. A friend battling infertility told me it took every ounce of courage she possessed to attend her friends' baby showers. Once, she was sitting in a circle of ladies at a shower, everyone focused on the mom-to-be, when another friend walked by and touched her shoulder in silent sympathy. She spent the rest of the evening crying in the bathroom, but she was grateful that someone had looked beneath her tissue-paper smile and recognized her pain.

Has anyone ever touched you like that? With a simple signal that says "I care"?

4. After Michael and Angel were married, he wanted to teach her what physical love should mean. But how could he do so?

> *"Do you still want to die?"*
>
> *"No, but I don't know why I want to live, either." The siege of emotion passed. Angel turned her head slightly and looked at him again. "Maybe it has something to do with you. I don't know anything anymore."*
>
> *Joy leaped inside Michael but only briefly. She looked hurt, not happy; confused, not certain. He wanted to touch her and was afraid if he did, she would take it the wrong way.*
>
> **Comfort my lamb.**
>
> If I touch her now, Lord . . .

Comfort your wife.
Michael took her hand.

God designed sex to be a meaningful part of marriage, but our culture has turned it into something else entirely. Why do you think God designed Adam and Eve as sexual beings? Has His intention for sex changed over the years? What does our society think about sex and the reasons for it?

5. Read the following scene of Angel being terrified by the realization that Michael wanted children. Why was she afraid? What secrets have you kept out of fear?

Michael should have children. He *wants* children.

Angel knew on Christmas night what she should do, but it was unbearable to even think of leaving him, of living without him. She wanted to stay here and forget the look in his eyes when he held Benjamin. She wanted to cling to him and bask in the happiness he gave her.

It was that very selfishness that made her realize she didn't deserve him.

Michael had given her everything. She had been empty, and he had filled her to overflowing with his love. She had betrayed him, and he had taken her back and forgiven her. He had sacrificed pride to love her. How could she discard his needs after that? How could she live with herself knowing that she had ignored the desires of his heart? What of Michael? What was best for him?

When Michael came in from the fields, she had a sumptuous venison dinner ready for him. The cabin was bedecked with flowers, the mantel, the table, the bed. Michael looked around bemused. "What are we celebrating?"

"Life," she said and kissed him. She drank in the sight of him, setting every angle of his face and body to memory. She wanted him desperately, loved him so much. Would he ever know how much? She couldn't tell him. If she did, he would come looking for her. He would bring her back. Better that he think her carnal and base. But she would have this last night to remember. He would be part of her no matter where she was and even if he never knew it. She would carry the sweet memories to her grave.

"Take me up to the hill again, Michael. Take me to the place where you showed me the sunrise."

He saw the hunger in her eyes. "It's cool tonight."

"Not too cold."

He could deny her nothing, but there was a strange uneasiness in the pit of his stomach. Something was wrong. He took the quilts from the bed and led the way. Perhaps she would talk to him and tell him what preyed on her mind. Maybe she would open up to him finally.

But her mood changed, swinging from pensive to abandoned. She ran to the top of the hill ahead of him and spun around, her arms spread wide. All around her, crickets sang, and the soft breeze stirred the grasses. "It's beautiful, isn't it? The vastness of it all. I'm utterly insignificant."

"Not to me."

"Yes," she said, turning to him. "Even to you." He frowned, and she turned again. "There shall be no other gods before me," she cried out to the heavens. "None but you, my lord." She turned and looked at him. None but you, Michael Hosea.

When she came close again, Michael caught hold of her. "Why are you doing this?"

"For you," she said, pulling his head down and kissing him.

Digging his fingers into her hair, he slanted his mouth across hers. He wanted to consume her. Her hands were like flame on his body.

God, I won't let her go again. I can't!

She moved against him, and he had no thought except for her, and it was not enough.

God, why are you doing this to me again? Do you give only to take away?

"Michael, Michael," she breathed, and he tasted the saltiness of his own tears on her cheeks.

"You need me." He could see her moonlit face. "You need me. Say it, Tirzah. Say it."

Let her go, beloved.

God, no! Don't ask it of me!

Give her to me.

No!

They clung to one another, seeking solace in sweet oblivion. But sweet oblivion doesn't last.

He closed his eyes against the fear uncurling in the pit of his stomach. I love her, Lord. I can't give her up.

Michael, beloved. Would you have her hung on her cross forever?

Lifting her, he held her cradled in his arms. She put her arm around his neck and kissed him. He closed his eyes. Lord, if I give her up to you now, will you ever give her back to me?

No answer came.

Angel had begun to love Michael and now saw things more clearly. Looking at him, she saw a man who stood with her when most other men would have cast her off. She saw a man who loved her as God loved her. She saw a man who wanted children, something she could never give him.

And that thought terrified her.

Three

FEAR

FEAR IS A UNIVERSAL feeling. Two of my experiences of being afraid stand out to me.

While in college, I went on a date with a handsome, charismatic young man. When we were alone, he boasted that he could kill me and no one would know. The look on his face gave me a jolt of instinctive fear. Flight was out of the question. He was bigger and faster than I. If I was going to escape, I'd have to fight with wits, not fists. I looked straight at him and said that everyone knew I was with him. The house where I lived had his name written in the ledger. My roommate expected me to return at a certain time.

He took me home.

The next time fear gripped my heart so thoroughly, I was on a road trip with three other women. We were following the Oregon Trail and looking for one specific site. We couldn't find it, so we pulled into a wayside park to study the map. A battered, dusty truck with two men inside pulled up next to us, rifles mounted in the back window. The men admired our Suburban and started a conversation. One of our ladies spilled the full story: four women on their own, more than a thousand miles from home and following the Oregon Trail. As she talked, the men exchanged a look. They claimed to know exactly where the site was and offered to lead us there. I tend to look people in the eye when they talk, and what I saw in theirs gave me chills.

As the driver, when we got back into the Suburban, I said I would follow them until they turned off. Then I intended to gun the engine and break the speed limit driving to the next town. Two of the women protested, saying they wanted to see the site and thought everything would be fine. The other woman sensed the same thing I did. So I hit the gas when the truck turned off the main road, and we hurtled past.

The next town had a historic house tour. While we were there, I asked the proprietor about the site we had planned to see. He said there was nothing on that side road to see. The place we were looking for was elsewhere and not worth seeing.

Instinctive fear is a gift from God to protect us from harm— even those who don't believe in Him.

Scripture proclaims that the beginning of knowledge is the fear of God (Proverbs 1:7). *Fear*, in this case, means "awe," or a comprehending of His omniscience, omnipresence, and omnipotence. He warns us of danger and can show us a way of escape. Sometimes we doubt, hesitate, or plunge ahead. Far too often I've chosen to do what seemed right in my own eyes. I trusted the wrong people, then distrusted those who had my best interests at heart. The world is so full of lies that it can be hard to know what the truth is, especially in our culture, where everyone has his or her own "truth."

The only love Angel had been exposed to was her mother's love—for her as a child but also for a self-serving man. Mae's love for Alex Stafford caused her to experience loss, abandonment, rejection, extreme poverty, a downward spiral into prostitution, the rise of shame, guilt, and ultimately death. Rab thought he was doing the right thing by selling Sarah to Duke. Sarah felt that God-given instinctive fear, but Duke immediately took away her identity and conditioned her to be abused, using that fear as a tool. She was so broken she came to believe she loved her captor. When she awakened to the truth about him, every escape attempt led to failure, disillusionment, and brutal punishment. Her last desperate attempt to break free took her around the Horn to California, where—hungry, beaten, and robbed, with no place to go—she surrendered to another ruthless captor, the Duchess.

After ten years as a sex slave, Angel locked her heart and mind in a cage of hate for those who bought and sold her, as well as for herself. Fear was her last protection. She numbed herself to survive the ongoing abuse. She didn't recognize truth because everyone she knew lied. She feared love because it had destroyed her mother. To Angel, *love* was synonymous with *misery* and *death*. She feared hope because it had always meant failure, disillusionment, and punishment.

After Michael took her from Pair-a-Dice to his cabin, she feared servitude. She had been a slave since the age of eight. Once she began to care for Michael, she feared her inadequacy. She had only one skill, and it wasn't one Michael intended to employ. Her life changed, but those changes left her feeling even more afraid. Like a wounded animal, she fought with everything in her.

Deep-seated fear makes it difficult to think straight. Fear prevents trust. The first time fear seizes us, it forms a link. Link by link, fear forges chains that hold us in bondage. No one can be free when fear is a constant companion.

Ironically, reverential fear of God can bring freedom. "Perfect love casts out fear" (1 John 4:18, NASB).

Knowing and believing that Jesus broke the chains of sin and death and that the almighty God loves us as His children dissolves fear.

God offers us what we have been longing for since the womb: real life and love that last forever.

The fears Angel held on to so tightly kept her from experiencing the blessings Michael offered. Only after his patience and tender wooing did she see the truth of things. Only then could she become free of the past and live abundantly in the present. She had to move past her fear to see how God could use the worst of her life experiences for His good purpose in her life—and for the freedom of other people.

You may have things in your past that have given you cause for fear, but you survived. God's light obliterates darkness. When we trust Him, He will make all things work together for His good purpose in our lives (Romans 8:28). When you face temptation again, He will show you a way to escape it (1 Corinthians 10:13).

Fear always comes knocking. Don't open the door.

Like a Seedling

We fear the thing we want the most.

OFTEN ATTRIBUTED TO ROBERT ANTHONY

ANGEL HAD SWORN *she would never love anyone, and now it was happening in spite of her. It stirred and grew against her will, pushing its way through the darkness of her mind to the surface. Like a seedling seeking the light of the spring sun, it came on. Miriam, little Ruth, Elizabeth. And now Michael. Every time she looked at him, he pierced her heart. She wanted to crush the new feelings, but still they came, slowly finding their way.*

Duke was right. It was insidious. It was a trap. It grew like ivy, forcing its way into the smallest cracks of her defenses, and eventually it would rip her apart. If she let it. If she didn't kill it now.

There's still a way out, *came the dark voice, counseling her.* **Tell him the worst of what you've done. Tell him about your father. That'll poison it. That will stop the pain growing inside you.**

So she decided to confess everything. Once Michael knew everything, it would be finished. The truth would drive a wedge in so deep between them, she would be safe forever.

Michael was chopping wood when she found him. He had his shirt off, and she stood silently watching him work. His broad back was already tanned, and hard muscles moved beneath the golden skin. He was power and beauty and majesty as he swung the ax in a wide arc, bringing it down hard, splitting the log clean through. The two halves banged off the block. As he bent to set up another, he saw her.

"Morning," he said, smiling. Her stomach fluttered. He looked pleased and surprised to see her watching him.

Why am I doing this?

Because you're living a lie. If he knew everything he would detest you and cast you out.

There's no reason for him to know.

Would you rather someone else told him? Then it will be even worse.

"I have to talk to you," she said weakly. All she could hear was the pounding of her heart in her own ears and that dark voice driving her on in desperation.

Michael frowned slightly. She was tense, worrying away at a gather in her skirt. "I'm listening."

Angel felt hot and cold all over. She should do it.

Yes. Do it, Angel.

She had to do it. Her palms were damp. Michael took his handkerchief from his back pocket and wiped the sweat from his face. When he looked at her, her heart sank.

I can't do it.

Yes, you can.

I don't want to.

Fool! You want to end up like your mother?

Michael studied her. She looked pale, small beads of perspiration breaking out on her forehead. "What's wrong? Are you feeling ill?"

Tell him and get it over with, Angel! It's what you really want, to make him let you go now while you can still bear it. If

you wait, it'll only hurt worse. He'll cut your heart out and carve it up for dinner.

"I've never told you the worst I've done."

His shoulders stiffened. "It's not necessary for you to confess everything. Not to me."

"You ought to know. You being my husband and all."

"Your past is your own business."

"Don't you think you should know what sort of girl you've got living with you?"

"Why the attack, Amanda?"

"I'm not attacking. I'm being honest.*"*

"You're pushing again. Pushing hard."

"You should know that—"

"I don't want to hear it!"

"—I had sex with my own father."

Michael let out a sharp breath as though she had punched him hard. He stared at her for a long moment, a muscle jerking in his cheek. "I thought you said he walked out of your life when you were about three."

"He did. He came back into it later, when I was sixteen."

Michael felt sick. God. God! Is there a sin this woman hasn't committed?

No.

And you ask that I love her?

As I have loved you.

Why had she done it? Why couldn't she keep some burdens on herself? "Did it make you feel better to throw that in my face?"

"Not much," she said dully. She turned and headed for the house, sickened at herself. Well, it was done. Finished. She wanted to hide. Her strides lengthened. She would pack a few things and be ready to leave.

Michael was shaking with anger. The idyll was over. The storm had hit.

As I have loved you, Michael. Seventy times seven.

More than anything, Angel feared love. Why? Because she was afraid of losing it. She believed what Duke had told her, that love was an insidious trap that would rip her apart. Angel was more scared of love than of death.

Fear is all about avoiding pain. We fear heights because we don't want to fall. We fear snakes because we don't want to get bitten. We fear fire because we don't want to get burned.

Even unusual fears are about avoiding pain. People who suffer from triskaidekaphobia—fear of the number thirteen—do so because they believe the number will bring bad luck. People who fear clowns—coulrophobes—are afraid of the evil that might be lurking behind clown masks. People who fear rabbits—leporiphobes—are afraid that bunnies will charge and bite them.

The cure for fear? Confidence—the confidence that springs from love.

A child learns to jump fearlessly from the edge of the pool into his father's arms because he knows Daddy will catch him. A child who doubts his father's willingness or ability will not be free from fear.

A young woman who prepares to play the piano for an audience of family members will not be frightened. Why? Because she knows they will not hurt her even if she makes a mistake. A professional pianist is not frightened because she is so confident in her ability that she does not worry about making mistakes.

The apostle John wrote,

> As we live in God, our love grows more perfect. So we will not be afraid on the day of judgment, but we can face him with confidence because we live like Jesus here in this world.

Such love has no fear, because perfect love expels all fear. If
we are afraid, it is for fear of punishment, and this shows that
we have not fully experienced his perfect love. We love each
other because he loved us first. (1 John 4:17–19)

Angel had no confidence in herself. She carried a heavy load of
guilt from her past and believed herself unworthy of love. Of course
she was afraid!

She was also afraid of the truth. Having worked as a prostitute,
she was comfortable with lies. Men had lied to her every day, and she
had returned those lies, measure for measure.

The pain of her past and the wounds from her childhood had
taught her that love results in destruction and that truth brings rejection.

Angel told Michael she never should have been born.

*Angel stared into the fire. "I'm not blind. I've had my eyes open all
my life. You don't think I know what I'm saying? You don't think
it's true? I heard my own father say I was supposed to be aborted."
Her voice broke. She regained control and went on more quietly.
"How can a man like you understand? My father was married.
He already had enough children. He told Mama she just wanted a
hold over him. I never knew if that was true. He sent her away.
He didn't want her anymore. Because of me. He stopped loving
her. Because of me."*

*She kept on in that quiet, agonized voice. "Mama's parents
were decent people in a good neighborhood. They wouldn't take
her in, not with an illegitimate child. Even her church turned her
away.*

*"We ended up on the docks," she said, emotionless now. "She
became a prostitute. When the men left, she'd drink herself to sleep
while Rab went out and drank the money away. She wasn't very
pretty anymore. She died when I was eight." She looked up at*

him. "Smiling." Her own mouth curved. "So you see. It is true. I
shouldn't have been born. It was all a terrible mistake from the
beginning."

With emotional trauma like Angel's, the worst part isn't what
happened. It's what hides within the emotional wound: the lie. The
lie is a conclusion that a person reaches through flawed logic—and
devoutly believes. The person tries to understand her experience
and usually concludes the fault somehow rests with her. The lie affects her concept of self-worth and makes it difficult for her to love,
trust, and live freely.[4]

Angel tried to explain her perspective to Michael:

"You want what I don't have. I can't love you. Even if I was able,
I wouldn't."

He hunkered down, took the damp blanket from her and cov-
ered her with the dry quilt. "Why not?"

"Because I spent the first eight years of my life watching my
mother do penance for loving a man."

Angel closed her eyes tightly. His desire for her would diminish
with time. He would stop loving her the same way her father had
stopped loving Mama. And if she let herself love Michael the way
Mama had loved Alex Stafford, he would tear her heart out.

I don't want to weep myself to sleep on a rumpled bed and
drink my life away.

Angel desperately needed two things: truth to replace the lies she
had been telling herself for years, and the ability to give and receive
love. God used Michael to teach her how to gain both, but it was a
difficult process because she had encased herself in protective armor.

However, like waves washing against the shore, love—consistent
and merciful—can wear away the hardest stone.

TO THINK ABOUT

1. What is your greatest fear? What sort of pain is involved in this fear, and what harm are you trying to avoid? Honestly, now—how likely is this fear to become reality?

2. What are some of the things Michael did to prove his love to Angel? Have you ever struggled to prove your love to someone who doubts it?

3. How does God demonstrate His love for us? What is the greatest thing He has ever done for us? What are some of the little things He does for everyone in order to demonstrate His love?

> When we were utterly helpless, Christ came at just the right time and died for us sinners. Now, most people would not be willing to die for an upright person, though someone might perhaps be willing to die for a person who is especially good. But God showed his great love for us by sending Christ to die for us while we were still sinners. (Romans 5:6–8)

4. Jesus told His disciples,

> *Don't be afraid* of those who threaten you. For the time is coming when everything that is covered will be revealed, and all that is secret will be made known to all. What I tell you now in the darkness, shout abroad when daybreak comes. What I whisper in your ear, shout from the housetops for all to hear!
> *Don't be afraid* of those who want to kill your body; they cannot touch your soul. *Fear only God,* who can destroy both soul and body in hell. What is the price of two sparrows—one copper coin? But not a single sparrow can fall to the ground without your Father knowing it. And the very hairs on your

head are all numbered. So *don't be afraid;* you are more valu-
able to God than a whole flock of sparrows. (Matthew 10:26–
31, emphasis added)

Jesus said we should fear . . . whom? Whom—or what—should
we not fear? Look at the italicized commands. We should not be
afraid of other people, even those who might want to harm us. We
should not be afraid of death. We should not be afraid of anything,
but we should have a reverential fear of God.

5. Why should we fear God? Consider these truths:

- The fear of the Lord is wisdom (Job 28:28; Psalm 111:10;
  Proverbs 9:10; 15:33).

- "The fear of the LORD is the beginning of knowledge"
  (Proverbs 1:7, NASB).

- "Fear of the LORD lengthens one's life" (Proverbs 10:27).

- "The fear of the LORD is a fountain of life" (Proverbs
  14:27, NASB).

- The fear of the Lord is our treasure (Isaiah 33:6).

- In the fear of the Lord is security (Proverbs 14:26).

- "Better to have little, with fear for the LORD, than to have
  great treasure and inner turmoil" (Proverbs 15:16).

- "Joyful are those who fear the LORD" (Psalm 112:1;
  128:1).

- To fear the Lord is to hate evil (Proverbs 8:13).

- The fear of the Lord will keep us from sinning (Exodus
  20:20).

- The fear of the Lord is our confidence (Job 4:6).

How could a proper fear of the Lord influence your life?
Wisdom can be defined as "seeing the world the way God sees it."

Knowledge is what we have learned through education and experience. Scripture tells us the fear of the Lord is wisdom *and* the beginning of knowledge. How is the fear of the Lord an important element in both?

If I speak with the tongues of men and of angels
but have not love,
> *I have become a noisy gong*
> *or a clanging cymbal.*

If I have the gift of prophecy
and know all mysteries and all knowledge,
and if I have all faith so as to remove mountains
but have not love,
> *I am nothing.*

If I give away all that I own
and if I hand over my body so I might boast
but have not love,
> *I gain nothing.*

Love is patient,
love is kind,
it does not envy,
it does not brag,
it is not puffed up,
it does not behave inappropriately,
it does not seek its own way,
it is not provoked,
it keeps no account of wrong,
it does not rejoice over injustice
> *but rejoices in the truth;*
it bears all things,

it believes all things,
it hopes all things,
it endures all things.

Love never fails—
but where there are prophecies,
    they will pass away;
where there are tongues,
    they will cease;
where there is knowledge,
    it will pass away.

For we know in part
and we prophesy in part;
but when that which is perfect has come,
    then that which is partial will pass away.

When I was a child,
    I spoke like a child,
    I thought like a child,
    I reasoned like a child.
When I became a man,
    I put away childish things.

For now we see in a mirror dimly,
    but then face to face.
Now I know in part,
    but then I will know fully,
    even as I have been fully known.

But now these three remain—
    faith, hope, and love.
    And the greatest of these is love. (1 Corinthians 13, TLV)

Never Enough

*No passion so effectually robs the mind of all its powers of
acting and reasoning as fear.*

EDMUND BURKE, *A PHILOSOPHICAL ENQUIRY INTO THE
ORIGIN OF OUR IDEAS OF THE SUBLIME AND BEAUTIFUL*

WHAT IF THE *Altmans did decide to stay in the valley? Angel massaged her throbbing temples. What did she have in common with them? Especially a young, doe-eyed virgin? When she had blurted out her past profession and how she and Michael had met, she had fully expected the girl to be shocked and leave her alone. The last thing she expected was that look of questioning concern and an offer of friendship.*

Angel felt movement beside her and opened her eyes against the pain in her head. Ruthie snuggled against her seeking warmth in her sleep. Her thumb had slipped out of her mouth. Angel touched the smooth pink cheek—and suddenly she saw Duke's enraged face swimming before her eyes. She felt the slap across her face again. "I told you to take precautions!" She could feel him grabbing her by her hair as he dragged her up from the bed so that his face was right in hers. "The first time was easy," he said through his teeth. "This time I'm going to make sure you never get pregnant again."

When the doctor came, she had kicked and fought, but it had done no good. Duke and another man strapped her to the bed. "Do it,"

Duke ordered the doctor and stood by watching to make sure he did. When she started to scream, they put a strap in her mouth. Duke was still there when the ordeal was over. Consumed in pain and weak from loss of blood, she'd refused to look at him.

"You'll be fine in a few days," he told her, but she knew she would never be all right. She called him the foulest name she knew, but all he did was smile. "That's my Angel. No tears. Just hate. It keeps me warm, my sweet. Don't you know that yet?" He kissed her hard. "I'll be back when you're better." He patted her cheek and left.

The black memory tortured Angel as she gazed at little Ruth Altman. She wanted desperately to leave the tent but was afraid if she got up she would awaken the others. Staring up at the canvas ceiling, she tried to think of something else. The rain started again, and with it came all her old ghosts.

"Can't sleep?" Michael whispered. She shook her head. "Turn on your side." When she did, he drew her back against him, tucking her into his body. The child shifted, snuggling deeper into the quilts and pressing into Angel's stomach. "You've got a friend," Michael murmured. Angel put her arm around Ruth and closed her eyes. Michael put his arm around both of them. "Maybe we'll have one like her someday," he said against her ear.

Angel stared into the fire in despair.

WITHIN A FEW *days, Elizabeth had a yellow plaid shirtwaist and rust skirt ready for fitting. Angel was hesitant to undress, embarrassed at the poor state of her worn undergarments. "It needs another tuck here, Mama," Miriam said, pulling in an inch at the skirtwaist.*

"Yes, and a little more fullness in the back, I think," Elizabeth said, fluffing the material at the back of the skirt.

Angel was disturbed that they would go to so much work on her behalf. The less they did, the less she would owe. "I'm going to be work-ing in the garden in these clothes."

"You needn't look like a drudge doing it," Miriam said.

"I don't want this to be a bother to you." *The dress was lovely as it was. It didn't need to be a perfect fit.*

"A bother?" Elizabeth said. "Nonsense. I haven't had so much fun in months! You can take the dress off now. Be careful of pins."

As Angel removed the dress and reached quickly for Tessie's worn clothing, she saw Elizabeth's pitying glance at the shabby camisole and threadbare pantalets. If she had her things from the Palace, these ladies would be impressed. They had probably never seen satin and lace un-dergarments from France, or silk wraps from China. Duke had dressed her only in the finest. Even Duchess, cheap as she had been, wouldn't have thought to dress her so crudely. But no, she had to appear to them in underwear made from used flour sacks.

She wanted to explain that the things weren't hers, that they be-longed to Michael's sister, but that would only raise questions she was loathe to answer. And worse, it might reflect badly on Michael. She didn't want them thinking ill of him. She didn't know why it mattered so much, but it did. She dressed quickly, stammered out a thank-you, and escaped to the garden.

MICHAEL CAUGHT ANGEL'S *shoulders.* "No. Let's talk about what's on your mind."

"There's nothing on my mind." *He waited, obviously unsatisfied, and she drew in a ragged breath.* "I knew better than to get close to them." *She pushed his hands away and hugged her shawl about her.*

"You think they love you less now that they're living in their own place?"

She glared at him defensively. "Sometimes I wish you'd just leave

*me alone, Michael. That you'd just send me back where I came from.
It'd be so much easier all the way around."*

"Because you're feeling *now?*"

"I felt *before,* and I got over it!"

"You adore Miriam and that little girl."

"So what?" *She would get over it, too.*

"What're you going to do when Ruth comes over here with another
fistful of mustard flowers? Show her the door?" *he asked harshly.* "She's
got feelings, too. So does Miriam." *He saw by her expression that she
didn't think they would come at all. He took her in his arms, holding
her there even when he felt her resistance.* "I've prayed unceasingly that
you might learn to love, and now you have. Only you fell in love with
them instead of me." *He laughed softly in self-mockery.* "There were
times when I wished I'd never brought them here. I'm jealous."

*Her cheeks burned, and she couldn't still her racing heart no mat-
ter how hard she tried. If he knew the power he had over her, what
would he do with it?* "I don't want to fall in love with you," *she said,
pushing away.*

"Why not?"

"Because you'll just end up using it against me." *She saw she had
angered him.*

"How?"

"I don't know. The truth is, maybe you wouldn't even know you're
doing it."

"Whose truth are we talking here? Duke's? *Truth sets you free.*
Were you ever free with him? Even for a single minute? He filled your
head with lies."

"And what about my father?"

"Your father was selfish and cruel. That doesn't mean every man in
the world is the same as him."

"Every man I've ever known is."

"Does that include me? What about John Altman? What about
Joseph Hochschild, and a thousand others?"

Her face jerked in pain.

Seeing her torment, he gentled. "You're a bird who's been in a cage all your life, and suddenly all the walls are gone, and you're in the wide open. You're so afraid you're looking for any way back into the cage again." He saw the emotions flicker across her pale face. "Whatever you choose to think now, it's not safer there, Amanda. Even if you tried to go back now, I don't think you could survive that way again."

He was right. She knew he was. She had reached the end of enduring it even before Michael claimed her. Yet, being here was no assurance.

What if she couldn't fly?

⤜❦⤏

Once Angel accepted her new life, she met the Altman family and developed relationships with the women—the mother, the teenage daughter, and the little girl. She cared for them and allowed them to touch her heart, though she did so reluctantly. Loving them was simple because these were nonsexual, nonthreatening relationships. These women were godly, wholesome, and skilled in domestic duties. They were everything Angel was not. Even though she was honest with them about her past, they loved and cherished her, and their love broke down her defenses.

Yet Angel was still afraid of being inadequate, especially when compared with the Altman women. She was especially afraid that she would never be able to give Michael the children he obviously wanted.

Life had been so much easier when the only person she had to think about was herself. Every day had been hard, but fearing only one thing—death at Magowan's hands—was easier than worrying about being inadequate, barren, and forever indebted to those who had given her so much love.

TO THINK ABOUT

1. The pain of infertility is especially hard for women in the childbearing years. A woman trying to get pregnant is likely to be surrounded by friends with bulging bellies.

The painful longing is intense, constant, and deeply personal for husband and wife. Angel felt that pain, coupled with guilt, and those desperate feelings fueled her fear that she would never be an adequate wife for Michael.

> There are three things that are never satisfied—
> no, four that never say, "Enough!":
> the grave,
> the barren womb,
> the thirsty desert,
> the blazing fire. (Proverbs 30:15–16)

Considering Angel's state of mind at that point, would she have been able to love God if she never bore a child? Would she ever have felt she was an appropriate wife for Michael? What would it take for her to acknowledge that Michael was the perfect husband for her?

2. When Elizabeth gifted Angel with lovely underwear, Angel's embarrassment involved far more than the worn condition of her flour-sack clothing. She was mortified to receive a gift given out of love. She did not believe she deserved Elizabeth's affection, and she didn't want to accept the gift any more than she wanted to receive Michael's love. If she could have, she would have negotiated an exchange of money or goods because she was unable to deal in emotional currency. She did not know how to repay Elizabeth with love from her own heart.

Have you ever felt humbled by a gift because you felt undeserving? How did you react to this gift? How do you wish you had re-acted?

3. Angel believed that loving and remaining with Michael would result in servitude—that she would be like her mama, who came to depend on her lover and whose life was destroyed when he cast her off. But Alex did not truly love Mae; he used her. His feeling for her was lust, not love.

Michael wanted to love Angel as God loves His children. Though the men who wrote the Bible often referred to themselves and others as "slaves of Christ," they counted themselves blessed.

Consider the following verses:

- In Philippians 1:1, Paul called himself a slave of Christ Jesus.

- First Corinthians 7:22 says, "Remember, if you were a slave when the Lord called you, you are now free in the Lord. And if you were free when the Lord called you, you are now a slave of Christ."

- Romans 6:19 explains our servitude this way: "Previously, you let yourselves be slaves to impurity and lawlessness, which led ever deeper into sin. Now you must give your-selves to be slaves to righteous living so that you will be-come holy."

- Galatians 1:10 says, "Obviously, I'm not trying to win the approval of people, but of God. If pleasing people were my goal, I would not be Christ's servant."

- Ephesians 6:6 says, "As slaves of Christ, do the will of God with all your heart."

- In James 1:1, James called himself "a slave of God and of the Lord Jesus Christ."

How should Christians feel about being slaves to Christ? Something in our human nature rises when we think about submitting our rights to someone else, but submitting them to our Lord and Creator? That's simple. It is our duty, and we are blessed to be used as His hands and feet on earth.

4. Michael taught Angel how to cook, plant, and tend a garden. The Altman women showed her how to sew. She picked up new skills every day. Should she have resented being asked to help out on Michael's farm? Was she working for her own good as well as his? How did her feelings about being a farmer's wife change as her love for Michael grew and deepened?

In the same way, the Holy Spirit teaches us every day if we are willing to listen. We learn how to read the Scriptures for greater understanding. We learn how to pray according to God's will instead of rattling off our list of wants and needs. We learn how to listen and minister to others. We learn how to endure temptation. We learn how to look forward to His coming and to anticipate our heavenly home.

How do our feelings about church, worship, and Bible study change as our love for the Lord grows and deepens?

5. John Donne wrote poetry in the seventeenth century. Although the world has changed since then, human emotions have not. One of his most beloved poems is "Batter My Heart, Three-Personed God," and in it he explored the contradictions involved in loving God. Angel could have written this sonnet, for in the same way John Donne battled God, she battled Michael, a representation of God. Emotionally weakened as he broke down her defenses with tenderness, she had been captured by love, her false beliefs exposed. She was beginning to love Michael but feared she was "married" to her past, Duke, and every other man who had ever mistreated her.

Angel finally realized that unless she was enthralled (in the seventeenth century, the word meant "enslaved") by Michael's love, she would never find true freedom. Likewise, she would never be pure unless she allowed herself to be ravished—fully and completely loved—by her husband.

Love overflows with paradoxes. We receive when we give; we find freedom when we surrender; we find joy when we confess our sins. Angel's fears robbed her of so much happiness. Has fear robbed you of joy? How can you banish that fear? Whom can you trust to handle that problem?

Batter my heart, three-personed God; for You
As yet but knock, breathe, shine, and seek to mend;
That I may rise, and stand, o'erthrow me, and bend
Your force, to break, blow, burn, and make me new.
I, like an usurped town to another due,
Labor to admit You, but oh! to no end;
Reason, Your viceroy in me, me should defend,
But is captived and proves weak or untrue.
Yet dearly I love You, and would be lovèd fain,
But am betrothed unto Your enemy.
Divorce me, untie, or break that knot again,
Take me to You, imprison me, for I
Except You enthrall me, never shall be free;
Nor ever chaste, except You ravish me.[5]

Mea Culpa

Hope is a dangerous thing. Hope can drive a man insane.
RED, FROM *THE SHAWSHANK REDEMPTION*,
SCREENPLAY BY FRANK DARABONT

ANGEL'S ONLY FRIEND *was a tired old harlot named Lucky, who was running to fat because of her thirst for brandy. Yet even Lucky knew nothing of where Angel had come from or been, or what had happened to make her the way she was. The other prostitutes thought of her as invulnerable. They all wondered about her, but they never asked questions. Angel made it clearly understood from the beginning that the past was sacred ground no one walked over. Except for Lucky, dumb-drunk Lucky for whom Angel held a fondness.*

Lucky spent her off time deep in her cups. "You gotta have plans, Angel. You gotta hope for something in this world."

"Hope for what?"

"You can't get by any other way."

"I get by just fine."

"How?"

"I don't look back, and I don't look forward."

"What about now? *You gotta think about now, Angel."*

Angel smiled faintly and brushed her long, golden hair. *"Now doesn't exist."*

NOTHING COULD BE *the same. Whatever might have grown between her and Michael was ruined. She knew that. The moment Paul had used her, she had thrown her last chance away.*

I did it to myself. I did it to myself. Mea culpa. Mea culpa.

Her mother's words haunted her, unbearable memories of a forsaken life. Why was she feeling this small light again when she knew it would only be destroyed in the end? Just as it always had been. Hope was cruel. Only the aroma of sustenance before a starving child. Not milk. Not meat.

Oh, God, I can't hope for anything. I can't. I won't survive if I do.

But it was there, a tiny spark glowing in the darkness.

AS SOON AS *the Altmans started off, Michael went to saddle his horse. Angel stood in the yard, watching the wagon roll away. She missed them already and could feel the gap widening like a chasm she couldn't cross. She kept remembering Mama sending her off with Cleo to the sea. She went into the house and packed a basket with sweet biscuits and winter apples. Nothing was going to be the same.*

Paul was at the cabin when the two of them arrived. He had a side of venison roasting on the spit. Angel hung up the curtains Elizabeth had made for Michael's cabin while the men talked. Michael went out to see if he could spot the Altmans yet. Angel felt Paul's cold gaze on her back.

"I bet they don't know anything about you, do they, Angel?"

She turned and faced him. He wouldn't believe the truth if she told him. "I like them very much, Paul, and I wouldn't want them to be hurt."

He sneered. "Meaning you hope I'll keep your sordid past a secret."

She saw it was no use appealing to him. "Meaning you'll do what you think you have to," she said dully. How long before he made them see her for what she really was? It would be very little time at all before they realized the animosity he held toward her, and they would wonder and ask why. What could she tell them? "He wanted me to pay for a ride, and I gave him the only currency I had"?

Why had she ever let herself get involved with these people? Why had she allowed herself to like them? She knew it was a mistake from the beginning.

"Love is debilitating," Sally had said.

"Have you ever been in love?" Angel had asked.

"Once."

"Who was it?"

"It's Duke." She gave a bitter laugh. "But I've always been too old for him."

A cold voice broke into her thoughts. "Scared, aren't you?" Paul's smile was stone cold. Angel went outside. She couldn't breathe in the cabin. The pain was beginning already. It was the same pain she felt the day she heard her father say he wished she had never been born, the same pain when Mama died, the same when she learned of Lucky's death. She had even felt pain the first time Duke gave her to another man.

Everyone to whom she drew close left her. Sooner or later they walked away. Or died. Or lost interest. Love someone, and it was a guarantee.

How could I forget what it felt like?

Because Michael fed you hope, and hope is deadly.

Sally told her once that you had to be like a stone because people would chip away at you, and that stone had to be big enough that they would never reach the very heart of you.

Angel saw Michael standing in the sunlight, strong and beautiful. Her heart twisted inside her. He of all of them had chipped away the most, and sooner or later, he would walk out of her life and leave a hole where her heart had been.

❧❧❧

A ngel thought something similar to the quote at the beginning of this section while working at Pair-a-Dice: "She preferred the numbness to this stirring of emotion. Hope was torment; hope was an enemy. And this man was a thorn in her side."

Angel feared many things: love, truth, inadequacy, servitude, and hope. Her entire life had been a nightmare from which she could not escape, though she had tried many times. Those attempts and failures taught her not to hope, because hope brought only more pain.

Gwen Purdie, author of *No More Hurting,* said it usually takes an outsider to help people like Angel:

Usually hope has to come from outside, because there is little hope left on the inside to work with. Help can be sought from family, friends, professionals or pastoral workers. In my experience of counseling those broken by sexual abuse, it is unusual for a person to deal with all the torn emotions and anguish which sexual abuse so often leaves behind without help of some kind. People often need compassionate and patient support in order to find the strength required to deal with their damaged innermost feelings and emotions. . . . Hope can also grow through understanding that there is a God who cares and has the power and will to help.[6]

Michael was the outsider God used to offer Angel a different way of life—a life with God at the center. Angel was not ready yet to hear about God—she barely trusted Michael—but Michael was not afraid to hope. He relied on hope to fulfill his role as her husband.

How many men would have let Angel go the first time she ran away? How many would have had the courage and selflessness to take her back after she'd had sex with Paul? How many would have forgiven her for the many times she turned away from love?

Michael was a godly man, but he was still human. He got angry and he felt hurt. He stormed and he wept. In his human nature, at one point he even wanted to kill Angel for frustrating him so deeply.

However, Michael was also wise enough to understand that human nature is low, corrupt, and selfish at its core. His spiritual nature led him to forgive, to seek after her, and to love. Most of all, through the long and arduous process of teaching Angel how to love, his spiritual nature compelled him to have hope. To have faith. To believe in a future that seemed far out of reach.

The psalmist put it this way: "O Lord, you alone are my hope" (Psalm 71:5).

TO THINK ABOUT

1. Hope stirred in Angel's heart by the midpoint of the book, but Michael's was filled with it. Why did he have hope? Why did he refuse to give up on Angel despite the many times she spurned his love?

2. Angel was learning to love Michael. Do you think he had to learn to love her, or was his love more instantaneous? How did he feed his love so it continued to strengthen? What prevented him from giving up?

3. What other characters in the story helped Angel grow and think of herself in a new light? Why do you think the Altmans appeared in the story? Why do you think Paul needed to be included?

4. Do you often feel hopeless?

Why am I discouraged?
   Why is my heart so sad?
I will put my hope in God!
   I will praise him again—
   my Savior and my God! (Psalm 42:5–6)

This psalm gives us step-by-step directions for overcoming hopelessness. The cure doesn't depend on us or our emotions. It depends on our confidence in God, whose love never fails.

5. Angel is not the only character who survived a rough childhood—Michael did as well. His cruel father rejected him. Michael suffered mental and physical abuse. But he told Angel he had learned to be grateful for his father because without that abuse he might never have come to know the Lord.

Michael's suffering wasn't as intense as Angel's, but he handled it by turning wholeheartedly to God, whereas Angel rejected Him. When you encounter suffering, which way will you turn?

"Amanda, I knew the day I saw you that you belonged with me."

"Do you know how many times men have said that to me?"
Angel said, wanting to drive him away.

Michael went on doggedly as though her words hadn't stabbed at him. "I've loved watching you grow and change. You're never the same. I love the way you take on new things, your drive to learn. I love how you work, how you have this little-girl look on your face when you finish something you've never tried before. I love watching you skip across the meadow with Ruth. I love seeing you laugh with Miriam and hang on Elizabeth's wisdom. I love the whole idea of growing old with you and waking up to you every morning for the rest of my life."

"Don't," she whispered brokenly.

"I haven't even started." He shook her tenderly. "Amanda, I loved giving you pleasure. I loved feeling you melt. I loved hearing you say my name." She blushed, and he kissed her. "Love cleanses, beloved. It doesn't beat you down. It doesn't cast blame." He kissed her again, wishing he had the right words to say what he felt. Words would never be enough to show her what he meant. "My love isn't a weapon. It's a lifeline. Reach out and take hold, and don't let go."

When he drew her into his arms this time, she didn't struggle. When she put her arms around him, he sighed, the stress of the past weeks dissolving. "This feels good, doesn't it? And right."

"I couldn't stop thinking about you," she said miserably, pressing closer, inhaling the sweet scent of his body. She had missed this feeling of safety that only came when she was with him. He was so determined to have her. Well, why not let him? Wasn't it what she wanted? To belong to him. To stay with him forever. Wasn't this what she had longed for every moment since she had left him?

"You make me hope, Michael. I don't know if that's good or not."

"It's good," he said, holding her close and rejoicing at her admission. It was a beginning.

Four

HUMILITY

H

UMILITY IS MORE EASILY recognized than defined.

My mother was a humble woman. Nursing was her calling. She worked full time at a VA hospital, on the terminal ward. When she came home from the hospital, she labored alongside my father, building our home from the foundation up, painting and decorating room by room. She wanted my brother and me to have benefits she and Dad never had. That meant spending what little extra money they had on church camps, Boy Scouts, swimming, dance and piano lessons, and road trips to as many national parks as they could pack into an annual two-week vacation. She had a small wardrobe: her uniform, work pants, and blouses she made. After she retired, she dedicated herself to church and community service. Once my father was diagnosed with terminal liver cancer, she took care of him at home. During his last hours, she sat behind him, her back against the headboard, so he could lean against her and breathe more easily until he passed away.

I don't remember my mother ever being idle, even on vacations.

She and I took long walks together. She wrote a trip journal, along with daily journals, cataloguing family events. Even her evenings were filled with ironing, knitting blankets, mending clothes, and writing letters. When I went away to college and later married, I received a handwritten letter every week. She wrote to family members and friends consistently. She wanted people to know they were loved and appreciated.

Humility is putting the needs of others before our own, acknowledging we don't have all the answers, knowing life is a journey with God as soul companion and guide, and paying attention to others without feeling the need to draw attention to ourselves. It's a sign of wisdom. A humble person is teachable, listens to others closely with sincere interest, and speaks truth with kindness.

A person who has self-control and serves others willingly without expecting praise shows humility. It takes meekness to accept and act on conviction and acknowledge that you are not always right and that you are a sinner in need of a Savior. A humble person leads by example, experiencing the love of God with a full and thankful heart. True humility springs from the life of Jesus Christ.

It took time for Angel to trust Michael, a humble man who lived for Christ. Once she knew she could trust him, she began to love him. From that love came the desire to serve him as a wife, to put his hopes and dreams ahead of her own. Michael wanted children, and Angel believed herself unable to have them. She mistakenly thought that if she removed herself from Michael's life, he would turn to Miriam, a loving girl who could give him children. When Angel left Michael for the last time, God made it clear he was not to go after her.

Angel grieved over her decision but believed she was doing the right thing. She thought she was on her own. Yet with every step, God made provision for her. Still she resisted. She followed each opportunity He gave with a thankful heart, though not fully aware of the One who guided her.

The enemy appeared and captured her again. In the old darkness, she remembered what Michael had taught her about God. Desperate for salvation for herself and others, she cried out to the Lord and He answered. Suddenly, miraculously free, she dared to believe. Her faith was a tiny mustard seed, but it grew strong as she was nurtured and encouraged by the people God put around her. With freedom came clarity; with clarity, purpose. Fledgling trust became love, then devotion and dedication to the God who had saved her. Her life was full in Christ. She was content. Everything seemed settled until God brought Paul to her door.

Humility means listening to God, obeying Him no matter how much it may hurt. We live in uncertainty until we take that first step of faith. God revealed the truth to Angel, but she had to make the choice to embrace and act on it.

Ultimately, humility leads to an abundant, joy-filled life in Christ . . . and that's what Angel found.

Born a Sinner

Before God can deliver us, we must undeceive ourselves.

SAINT AUGUSTINE

WHEN ANGEL LOOKED *up, she saw Michael standing in a field. The soft wind made the wheat look like a golden sea around him. The air was sweet and clean. Miriam was walking toward him, a baby in her arms, but he paid her no attention. "Amanda!" he called out, running toward her.*

"No, Michael, go back! Don't come near me!" She knew if he touched her, the foulness covering her would cover him as well. "Stay away! Stay back!"

But he would not listen. He came ahead.

She was too weak to run away. She looked down at herself and saw her flesh decaying and dropping away. Michael walked toward her without hesitation. He was so close, she could see his eyes. Oh . . . "God, let me die. Let me die for him."

No, *came a soft voice.*

She looked up and saw Michael standing before her. A small flame burned where his heart was. ***No, beloved.*** *His mouth hadn't moved, and the voice was not his. The flame grew larger and brighter, spread-*

ing until his entire body was radiant with it. Then the light separated from Michael and came the last few feet toward her. It was a man, glorious and magnificent, light streaming from him in all directions.

"Who are you?" she whispered, terrified. "Who are you?"

Yahweh, El Shaddai, Jehovah-mekoddishkem, El Elyon, El Olam, Elohim . . .

The names kept coming, moving together like music, rushing through her blood, filling her. She trembled in fear and could not move. He reached out and touched her, and she felt warmth encompassing her and the fear dissolving away. She looked down at herself and found she was clean and clothed in white.

"Then I am dead."

That you may live.

Blinking, she looked up again and saw the man of light covered with her filth. "No!" she wept. "Oh, God, I'm sorry. I'm so sorry. I'll take it back. I'll do anything . . ." Yet even as she reached out, the defilement disappeared and he stood before her perfect again.

I am the way, Sarah. Follow me.

As she stepped forward and reached out for him, there was a thunder clap, and Angel awakened in darkness.

Finding herself in Duke's custody again, Angel yearned for Michael—for his love, his forgiveness, his comforting presence. Overcome by shame, she carried that feeling into her dreams, where everything Michael had ever said culminated in a vision. Angel saw herself as she was—a human covered in the filth of sin—and then a shining man appeared who dared to take her sin on Himself.

Have you ever really considered what that means? "Every sin" means every evil thought I've had over my lifetime and every sinful deed, even good deeds tainted with a measure of pride. And not just *my* sin, but every sin of every human being from Adam and Eve to the last man and woman standing on earth. I can't get through a day without something flitting through my mind that leaves me thinking, *Where did* that *come from? How did* that *get into my head?* I surely fail to understand a fraction of the anguish and suffering Jesus experienced in the Garden of Gethsemane, the burden He carried to the cross, and what it took to remain hanging there until death.

Guilt results when we feel bad about something we've done. Shame, on the other hand, is a stronger emotion because the problem is not disobedience; the problem is *us*. We can't be perfect or holy no matter how hard we try.

Mary of Magdala, better known as Mary Magdalene, traveled with Jesus during His three years of ministry. We don't know much about her background, but we can draw some conclusions from Scripture.

The place Magdala was a primarily Gentile city well known for trade. It was famous for dyed fabrics and salted fish, and Gentiles came from miles around to shop in its market. Tradition holds that Mary Magdalene was a prostitute, but no biblical evidence supports that supposition. Scripture tells us she was possessed by seven demons and that Jesus cast the demons out of her (Luke 8:2).

How did she come to be possessed? Perhaps she had opened herself to the demons by hiring a fortune-teller or an astrologer to read her future in the stars. (Such things were forbidden by Jewish law.) Or she might have had a tragedy in her life. Perhaps she had lost her husband, her child, or both. Maybe she had been abused, assaulted, or abandoned. In any case, something had happened to her—something tragic enough to make her abandon God and everything she'd been taught by the rabbi. She turned from Adonai to another power, and seven demons entered her.

The demons likely ruined her life. When they were in charge, she could be violent, rude, and abusive. If she had a family, they probably cast her out, and she might have even been cast out of her city. She might have roamed the countryside like a madwoman until she came upon Jesus and His followers as they stopped at a well.

Jesus saw Mary Magdalene and understood her problem at once. Despite the ravings of the demons, who must have recognized Him, Jesus put out His hand and commanded them to leave her. After they had gone, Mary stood before Him, stunned, blinking, and clean. Forgiven of her sins, forgiven for turning away from God. Forgiven for her doubt and anger.

Grateful beyond words, she followed Him . . . that day and every day of His ministry. The Bible tells us she and several other women gave of their own fortunes to support His work (Luke 8:2–3). They may have done the cooking, cleaning, and mending of torn garments as Jesus and His disciples traveled throughout Galilee and Judea. While the women worked, they listened at the feet of the Master and heard of a new way of following God. They learned that entering the kingdom of God was a matter not of keeping a set of rules but of living with God as the King of their lives. "The Kingdom of God," Jesus said, "is already among you" (Luke 17:21).

When Jesus—the sinless Son of God, who took on Himself every sin committed by every man, woman, and child in the world—died on the cross, Mary was nearby, watching the horror. She was there when they took Him down from the cross, and she went with Nicodemus and Joseph of Arimathea when they placed Jesus in a borrowed tomb. She made note of the location because she and the other women planned to go again on the first day of the week to finish anointing the body for burial.

On that Sunday morning, after the sun had crested the eastern horizon, Mary Magdalene was the first to see the risen Jesus. Some say she was the first missionary because she went and "told the disciples that she had seen the Lord, and that He had spoken these things to her" (John 20:18, NKJV).

Before we can realize we need someone to save us from our sin, we must realize we are sinners. Few people talk about sin today, but it's an ever-present problem whether we admit it or not. So many things that used to be considered sinful no longer are, but the Word of God is clear and uncompromising: anything we do contrary to the will of God is sin. It could be something as small as overeating (the sin of gluttony) or an action as destructive as adultery. It could be holding a grudge against a neighbor or stealing from an employer. Even knowing what is right and not doing it is sin (James 4:17).

Angel had no problem seeing herself as a sinner—after all, she was a prostitute, and people like Paul weren't shy about calling prostitution a shameful sin, even though he had no problem using her as a prostitute when it suited him. Other people, however, do occasional good deeds and consider themselves good people.

Yet compared with God's holiness, our goodness looks like a pile of filthy rags (Isaiah 64:6) because the good we do could never overcome the sins we have done or will do. Romans 3:23–24 tells us, "Everyone has sinned; we all fall short of God's glorious standard. Yet God, in his grace, freely makes us right in his sight. He did this through Christ Jesus when he freed us from the penalty for our sins."

Humans are sinful because we are born with a sinful nature. We don't have to be taught how to be selfish; that urge comes naturally. We need to learn how to be good, and we must accept Christ's redemption if we want to be completely clean.

The good news is that we *can* be completely clean—because Jesus's blood "cleanses us from *all* sin" (1 John 1:7, emphasis added).

Is there an unforgivable sin? Some people become anxious when they read about what happens with blasphemy of the Holy Spirit: "'I tell you the truth, all sin and blasphemy can be forgiven, but anyone who blasphemes the Holy Spirit will never be forgiven. This is a sin with eternal consequences.' [Jesus] told them this because they were saying, 'He's possessed by an evil spirit'" (Mark 3:28–30).

The issue in this passage isn't so much a matter of language as it is *mindset.* Jesus was speaking to a group of religious leaders who observed His miracles, rejected them, and then went so far as to attribute them to Satan. They witnessed the work of the Holy Spirit and stubbornly set their minds against it.

The only unforgivable sin is to reject the free gift of salvation through Jesus Christ and the conviction of His Holy Spirit.

TO THINK ABOUT

Hamartiology—there's a word you don't use every day. It's a theological term referring to the doctrine of sin, and it comes from the Greek word *hamartia,* which means "missing the mark."[7] Since the average man or woman on the street today does not think much about sin, maybe we should review what sin is and how serious its consequences are.

1. *Sin is a transgression of God's law.*

In the Garden of Eden, Adam and Eve had only one law to obey: don't eat from the tree of the knowledge of good and evil. After they broke that law, God gave them other laws to help them understand His standard of holiness. He had to spell things out. He had to say, "Don't have other gods before Me. Don't murder. Don't sleep with your neighbor's husband. Don't bear false witness against anyone."

"The law always brings punishment on those who try to obey it. (The only way to avoid breaking the law is to have no law to break!)" (Romans 4:15).

Though we are no longer under the Mosaic law, the Bible is filled with other warnings about God's standard of holiness. Jesus said that nursing feelings of hatred in our hearts is sinful (Matthew 5:21–22).

So, how do we avoid disobeying God's directions? We study His Word so we can understand what sin is.

Take your notebook and jot down every sin you can name. It might help if you classify them into sins of commission (things we do), sins of omission (things we should do but don't), and sins of attitude.

What does the average person think about sin? Is it an old-fashioned idea? Why is it still relevant? When did you realize you are a sinner? Have you experienced the forgiveness of Jesus Christ? How does being forgiven change your perspective of other people?

2. *Sin can be doing something right for the wrong reason.*

Suppose you are going out to eat with a friend who is a recovering alcoholic. You have no problem with wine; you have a glass with dinner on occasion. Should you order a glass when you dine with your friend?

The Bible addresses this question:

> Remember, all foods are acceptable, but it is wrong to eat
> something if it makes another person stumble. It is better not
> to eat meat or drink wine or do anything else if it might cause
> another believer to stumble. You may believe there's nothing
> wrong with what you are doing, but keep it between yourself
> and God. Blessed are those who don't feel guilty for doing
> something they have decided is right. But if you have doubts
> about whether or not you should eat something, you are sin-
> ning if you go ahead and do it. For you are not following your
> convictions. If you do anything you believe is not right, you
> are sinning. (Romans 14:20–23)

Insisting on your right to drink wine in front of your alcoholic friend is selfish and demonstrates a lack of love. That's sin.

In what other situations could this principle apply? What about in the area of modesty? Should you wear a sexy outfit in the company of a man who is not your husband? You may have the right to wear what you choose, but are you insisting on your right to the detriment of someone else?

3. *Repeated sin hardens us against God.*

Hebrews 3:13 admonishes us, "You must warn each other every day, while it is still 'today,' so that none of you will be deceived by sin and hardened against God." And Ephesians 4:18 says this about those who continue in sin: "Their minds are full of darkness; they wander far from the life God gives because they have closed their minds and hardened their hearts against him."

The first time we commit a sin, our guts warn us against it. The next time we do the same thing, the warning is slighter. The next time is even less painful. The more we do it, the less we cringe; we may even celebrate our success, bragging about what we managed to pull off.

Sin builds a wall between us and God. We saw this wall in Angel's life, and it took Michael (and God!) a long time to bring that wall down. Have you felt convicted about your engagement in some activity? What is it?

If you find yourself defending this activity, you've become hardened in that area. It's time to take a fresh, hard look at your life: Does your involvement in this activity please God? If the answer is no, you need to stop. Cold turkey.

You'll be on your way to tearing down the barrier between you and God, who wants the best for you.

4. *We are tempted to sin by three things: our physical appetites, our eyes, and pride.*

Do not love this world nor the things it offers you, for when
you love the world, you do not have the love of the Father in

you. For the world offers only a craving for physical pleasure, a craving for everything we see, and pride in our achievements and possessions. These are not from the Father, but are from this world. (1 John 2:15–16)

You need only watch TV for an hour to see confirmation of these verses. Craving for physical pleasure? A new car being sold by a sexy man and woman using subtle appeals to physical pleasure: the soft leather seats, the new-car smell, the expensive stereo, the rumble of the engine. Check. Craving for what we see? The furniture store ad with the plush designer sofa, the big mountain house with endless windows and expansive views. Check. Pride? You can own this and that. You can be the woman with the gorgeous hair. You can be proud of your new body, cars, shoes, job . . . Check.

Do any of these things have eternal significance? Will any of them last forever? Will any of them please God?

Only you can answer those questions. The items in those commercials are designed to please you, to satisfy your cravings for things you may not *need* but can be persuaded to desperately *want*.

It is not sinful to have nice things if the Lord allows you to have them. Sin occurs when you stop listening to God and start pursuing *possessions* at all costs—when you spend money you don't have to acquire them or when you can't care for your family because you've spent everything to obtain what your fleshly nature desires.

The next time you watch TV, detach for a moment and notice how the commercials—and many shows—are designed to persuade you. Some want you to spend your money. Some want you to change your mind about a social issue. Others want to convince you that hedonistic lifestyles are perfectly acceptable.

What commercials or shows come to mind?

Consider these appeals carefully, and harden your heart against anything that contradicts the Word of God.

5. Consider the following psalm, which David wrote after being confronted about his sin with Bathsheba. Have you ever felt like David? What sins have made you beg God for mercy and cleansing?

Have mercy on me, O God,
because of your unfailing love.
Because of your great compassion,
blot out the stain of my sins.
Wash me clean from my guilt.
Purify me from my sin.
For I recognize my rebellion;
it haunts me day and night.
Against you, and you alone, have I sinned;
I have done what is evil in your sight.
You will be proved right in what you say,
and your judgment against me is just.
For I was born a sinner—
yes, from the moment my mother conceived me.
But you desire honesty from the womb,
teaching me wisdom even there.

Purify me from my sins, and I will be clean;
wash me, and I will be whiter than snow.
Oh, give me back my joy again;
you have broken me—
now let me rejoice.
Don't keep looking at my sins.
Remove the stain of my guilt.
Create in me a clean heart, O God.
Renew a loyal spirit within me.

Do not banish me from your presence,
  and don't take your Holy Spirit from me.

Restore to me the joy of your salvation,
  and make me willing to obey you.
Then I will teach your ways to rebels,
  and they will return to you. (Psalm 51:1–13)

The Choice to Surrender

*Wherever God rules over the human heart as King, there
is the kingdom of God established.*

PAUL W. HARRISON

EACH SUNDAY FOLLOWING *the sermon, the pastor gave an invitation to anyone wanting to receive Christ as their Savior and Lord. Each time he gave the opportunity to come forward, Angel felt her nerves tighten.*

The still, quiet voice beckoned tenderly.

Come to me, beloved. Stand and come to me.

Warmth swept over her. This was the love she'd been waiting for all her life. Yet she could not move. Oh, Michael, if only you were with me today. If only you were here to walk forward with me, maybe then I'd have the courage.

Each Sunday, she closed her eyes, trying to gather her nerve to answer the call—and each Sunday she failed to do it. She sat trembling, knowing she was unworthy, knowing that after all she had said against God, she had no right to be his child.

On the fourth Sunday, Susanna leaned close and whispered, "You want to go forward, don't you? You've wanted to for weeks."

Eyes stinging, throat closed tight, Angel nodded once and hung her head, her lips pressed together. She was afraid, so afraid she was shaking. What right had she to present herself to God and receive mercy? What right?

"I'll walk with you," Susanna said and took her hand firmly.

It was the longest walk of Angel's life as she went down the aisle and faced the pastor waiting at the end of it. He was smiling, his eyes shining. She thought of Michael and felt a rush of anguish. Oh, Michael, I wish you were here with me now. I wish you were here to see this. Will you ever know you struck the match and brought light into my darkness? *Her heart filled with gratitude.* Oh, God, he loves you so.

She didn't cry. She had years of practice containing her emotions, and she wouldn't give in to them now before all these people, not even with Susanna Axle at her side. She could feel the eyes of everyone in the church upon her, watching her every move, listening for any catch in her voice. She mustn't make a fool of herself.

"Do you believe that Jesus is the Christ, the Son of the Living God?" the pastor asked her.

"I believe," she said with grave dignity and closed her eyes briefly. Oh, God, forgive my unbelief. Make my faith larger than a mustard seed, Jesus. Let it grow. Please.

"And do you give your life to Jesus now before these witnesses? If so, would you signify by saying I do?"

Words meant for a wedding ceremony. A sad smile touched her lips. With Michael she had said "Why not" rather than "I do"; she had come to the end of her endurance and felt she had no choice. She felt that now. She had come to the end of her struggles, the end of her fight to survive on her own. She needed God. She wanted him. He had brought her out of her old life when she had no faith. And now that she knew he really was there, he was holding out his hand to her and making a proposal.

Oh, Michael, this is what you wanted for me, isn't it? This is what you meant when you said someday I'd have to make a choice.

"Angel?" the pastor said, perplexed. No one breathed or moved.

"I do," she responded, smiling radiantly. "I most assuredly do."

He laughed. Turning her toward the congregation, he said, "This is Angel. A new sister in Christ. Welcome her."

And they did.

After living with the Axle family for a while, Angel realized she had entered a different world—a world where people cared about others, where God was the focus of daily life. The Axles were like Michael, and being around them only made Angel miss Michael more. She felt a bit like a stranger in a strange land.

The Bible tells the story of Ruth, another woman who felt that way. Elimelech and Naomi moved their family to Moab to escape a famine in Judah, and Ruth married one of their sons. They all lived together in Moab ten years. During that time Naomi's husband and sons died, leaving her with the two daughters-in-law, Ruth and Orpah. Once the famine in Judah ended, Naomi packed up her household and set out for home with the young women.

On the way, Naomi had second thoughts and said,

> "Go back to your mothers' homes. And may the LORD reward
> you for your kindness to your husbands and to me. May the
> LORD bless you with the security of another marriage." Then
> she kissed them good-bye, and they all broke down and wept.
> (Ruth 1:8–9)

After initially protesting, Orpah went back to Moab, but Ruth remained with her mother-in-law. She told Naomi,

> Don't ask me to leave you and turn back. Wherever you go, I
> will go; wherever you live, I will live. Your people will be my
> people, and your God will be my God. Wherever you die, I

will die, and there I will be buried. May the LORD punish me
severely if I allow anything but death to separate us! (verses
16–17)

Though Naomi was well past childbearing age, Ruth was still a
young woman. Naomi wanted Ruth to be happy, to have a family
of her own, but Ruth was so determined that Naomi should not be
abandoned that she sacrificed her right to remain in her own land
among her own people. Like Angel, she was about to enter a different world, one where God was the invisible member of every household and the focus of people's lives.

The people of Israel were religious; however, they were not on
good terms with Ruth's people, the Moabites. Though the people of
Moab were descended from Lot, Abraham's nephew, they were one
of two tribes that refused Israel safe passage through their land after
the Hebrews left Egypt. Instead, the Moabites hired Balaam, son of
Beor, to curse the Israelites. God noted their hostility and later de-
creed that no Moabite or Moabite descendant for ten generations
could enter the assembly of the Lord (Deuteronomy 23:3).

As Ruth traveled with Naomi, she must have wondered how she
would be received. She was not Hebrew, she probably spoke a different language, and since people enjoy nothing more than a juicy
story, she would certainly be gossiped about as a newcomer. Some
people would be prejudiced against the Moabites, for people have
long memories.

When the two women arrived in Bethlehem, Naomi's hometown, all the women who remembered her said, "Can this be
Naomi?"

"Don't call me Naomi," she responded. "Instead, call me Mara,
for the Almighty has made life very bitter for me. I went away
full, but the LORD has brought me home empty. Why call
me Naomi when the LORD has caused me to suffer and the
Almighty has sent such tragedy upon me?" (Ruth 1:20–21)

The women of Bethlehem probably spent the next few weeks gossiping about why God had taken Naomi's husband and sons. Had they been sinning? Had their faith in the God of Israel been so weak they were punished for fleeing to Moab? And what of that woman who came back with Naomi? Was she like the Moabites who had refused to help the children of Israel?

After they settled in Bethlehem, Ruth and Naomi faced the critical problem of supporting themselves. They arrived during the barley harvest. Long before, God had commanded the Israelites to leave grain in the fields for the poor (Leviticus 23:22). Knowing that the women of the town were suspicious of her, Ruth asked Naomi for permission to go into the nearby fields and gather the leftover grain. Naomi allowed her to go, and Ruth gleaned in a field that happened to belong to Boaz, a man from her late father-in-law's family.

Boaz's background is never mentioned in the biblical book of Ruth, but it is remarkable. His mother, Rahab, was a former harlot from Jericho who saved two Israelite spies. Rahab and her family were spared when the Israelites destroyed the famous walled city (Joshua 2; 6:22–25). She married a Hebrew named Salmon, and together they had Boaz (Matthew 1:5).

So Boaz, of mixed-race parentage, must have encountered some degree of prejudice or suspicion during his lifetime. When he spotted Ruth working in his field, he asked his foreman, "Whose young woman is this?" (Ruth 2:5, TLV).

The man replied, "She is a Moabite woman who came back with Naomi from the region of Moab" (verse 6, TLV). He explained that she'd labored all morning, taking only a short break in the shelter.

Boaz called Ruth over and told her to remain in his field and not to worry about her safety because he had ordered the young men to leave her alone. He told her to help herself from the water jars and take as much grain as she needed.

Ruth fell to the ground, bowing before him. "Why have I found favor in your eyes that you have noticed me, even though I am a foreigner?" (verse 10, TLV).

Boaz said, "All that you have done for your mother-in-law since your husband's death has been fully reported to me—how you left your father and mother and the land of your birth, and came to a people you did not know before. May ADONAI repay you for what you have done, and may you be fully rewarded by ADONAI, God of Israel, under whose wings you have come to take refuge" (verses 11–12, TLV).

After that, Naomi played matchmaker. Since God had established rules that allowed a relative to protect his extended family by redeeming land, freeing the enslaved, serving as a trustee, and providing an heir, Naomi gave Ruth explicit instructions: she should bathe and perfume herself, put on her cloak, and go down to the threshing floor, where Boaz would spend the night. After he fell asleep, Ruth was to lie down at his feet and remain there until he woke. He would then tell her what to do.

When Boaz woke and found Ruth at his feet, he remembered his obligation as a kinsman-redeemer. "May you be blessed by ADONAI, my daughter!" he said. "You have made the latter act of loyalty greater than the first, by not running after the young men, whether rich or poor" (3:10, TLV).

Ruth learned that Adonai was a loving God, one who cared about His people, including foreigners who accepted Him. God made provision for her by commanding the people to leave grain in the fields, and He redeemed her situation through the practices He had instituted that would not leave widows unprotected.

After making certain that another kinsman-redeemer did not wish to exercise his right, Boaz married Ruth and they had Obed, a son. He would be the father of Jesse, who would be the father of David. And generations later, both Joseph and Mary would be descendants of Ruth and Boaz. Mary was the mother of Jesus, the Son of God.

TO THINK ABOUT

1. Angel finally found the courage to accept Jesus as her God and Savior. She believed wholeheartedly. What do you suppose Ruth felt when she placed her faith in a different God? What did she have to accept when she moved to Bethlehem with Naomi?

2. What do you think Boaz loved about Ruth? In those days, love usually came after marriage, but Boaz treated Ruth tenderly and with great respect before she approached him at the threshing floor. What qualities do you think he saw in her? Why do you think he was so pleased to awaken and see her lying at his feet?

3. The term *kinsman-redeemer* does not apply to only the people of Israel. In a sense, God is *our* kinsman-redeemer (Isaiah 44:24), determined to protect His relationship with His people. He is our "next of kin," who ransoms us from the bondage of sin (43:1–3).

Until Michael came along, Angel had a distorted view of God. She believed He was unmerciful, a God who enjoyed inflicting pain. How could she see Him as a loving kinsman-redeemer when the only father she had ever known wanted her ripped out of her mother's womb and thrown away?

Boaz had to pay a price to redeem Ruth and marry her. How did God pay a price to set us free? What should be our reaction to our kinsman-redeemer? How has He provided for you?

4. If you are a Christian, can you remember the time when you surrendered your will to Christ and gave Him control of your life? How was your experience compared with Angel's?

If you are not a Christian, have you ever considered surrendering your life to Christ? If you are not sure, what is holding you back?

5. Ruth became part of Boaz's family when he redeemed and married her. When we accept Christ, we are adopted into His family and become part of the bride of Christ, the church.

All who are led by the Spirit of God are children of God.

So you have not received a spirit that makes you fearful slaves. Instead, you received God's Spirit when he adopted you as his own children. Now we call him, "Abba, Father." For his Spirit joins with our spirit to affirm that we are God's children. And since we are his children, we are his heirs. In fact, together with Christ we are heirs of God's glory. But if we are to share his glory, we must also share his suffering. (Romans 8:14–17)

Now that we are part of Christ's family, what benefits do we have? How does it feel to be part of a huge, loving family? We are also heirs; what will we inherit?

Can we give up all for the love of God? . . .
    If with courage and joy we pour ourselves out for Him and for others for His sake, it is not possible to lose, in any final sense, anything worth keeping. We will lose ourselves and our selfishness. We will gain everything worth having.[8]

Redemption

*When you find your definitions in God, you find the very
purpose for which you were created. Put your hand into
God's hand, know His absolutes, demonstrate His love,
present His truth, and the message of redemption and
transformation will take hold.*

RAVI ZACHARIAS

ANGEL KNEW THE *moment Michael saw her. He glanced up as she
was crossing the meadow. He stood very still, staring at her in the distance.*

I mustn't cry. I mustn't.

*She kept walking toward him. He didn't move. Doubt stirred
again, but she fought it down. She wanted to shed all the barriers that
had kept her from him, all those months of defiance and fear and
uncertainty. She wanted to discard the horrible memories of her childhood and the guilt she had taken on herself for things she had been
powerless to stop.*

*If only things had been different. She wanted so desperately to be
clean for him, to be new. She wanted to please him. She would give the
rest of her life to that end if he would let her. She wanted to strip away
her past. Oh, if she could only be Eve again, a new creature in Paradise. Before the Fall.*

With trembling hands, she removed the trappings of the world. She dropped her shawl and took off the woolen jacket. She worked at the tiny buttons of the shirtwaist. She shrugged it off and let it drop as she walked. She unhooked her skirt and let it slide down over her hips and to the ground. She stepped out of it.

Without faltering, she walked toward him.

Lord, no matter what he does or says, I have to thank him. He was always your good and faithful servant, and I never thanked him. Not enough. Oh, God, never, never enough.

She removed the camisole and slips, the corset cover and corset and pantalets. With each garment she removed and dropped, she cast away anger, fear, and her blindness to the multitudes of joy in life, her own desperate pride. She had one single, abiding purpose: to show Michael she loved him, and she peeled away the layers of pride one by one until she was humbled by her own nakedness. Last of all, she stepped out of her thin leather shoes and drew the pins that held her hair.

As she came close, she saw the gray at his temples and the new lines in his beloved face. When she looked into his eyes, everything she felt spilled over. She had always known her own pain and loneliness, her own need. Now she came to face his.

Oh, what had she done to him in denying her love, in turning away? She had played God and done what she thought best for him, and all she had done was cause him pain. She thought he was too strong to be hurt, too wise to wait. How much had her martyrdom cost him?

All her carefully planned words fled. So many words to say a simple, heartfelt thing: I love you, and I'm sorry. *She could not even speak. The tears that had been frozen inside her all her life came, and the last bastion melted away in a flood.*

Weeping, Angel sank to her knees. Hot tears fell on his boots. She wiped them away with her hair. She bent over, heartbroken, and put her hands on his feet. "Oh, Michael, Michael, I'm sorry . . ."

Oh, God, forgive me.

She felt his hand on her head. "My love," *he said. He took hold of her and drew her up again. She couldn't look into his face, wanting to hide her own. Michael took off his shirt and put it around her shoulders. When he tipped her chin up, she had no choice but to look into his eyes again. They were wet like hers but filled with light. "I hoped you would come home someday," he said and smiled.*

"There's so much I have to say. So many things to tell you."

He combed his fingers into her flowing hair and tilted her head back. "We have the rest of our lives."

She knew then that she had doubted he would forgive her again, but he already had. She could live with him forever and not know his depths. Oh, Lord, thank you, thank you! *She went into his arms, spreading her hands on his strong back, pressing herself as close as she could, her gratitude so strong she could hardly bear it. He was warmth and light and life. She wanted to be flesh of his flesh, blood of his blood. Forever. Closing her eyes, she inhaled the sweet scent of him and felt she was finally home again.*

She thought she had been saved by his love for her, and in part she had been. It had cleansed her, never casting blame. But that had been only the beginning. It was loving him in return that had brought her up out of the darkness. What can I give him more than that? I would give him anything.

"Amanda," Michael said, holding her tenderly. "Tirzah . . ."

Sarah, *came the still, soft voice, and she knew the one gift she had to offer. Herself. Angel drew back from Michael and looked up at him. "Sarah, Michael. My name is Sarah. I don't know the rest of it. Only that much. Sarah."*

Michael blinked. His whole body flooded with joy. The name fit her so well. A wanderer in foreign lands, a barren woman filled with doubt. Yet Sarah of old had become a symbol of trust in God and ultimately the mother of a nation. Sarah. A benediction. Sarah. A barren woman who conceived a son. His beautiful, cherished wife who would someday give him a child.

He held out his hand. "Hello, Sarah." She looked endearingly con-

fused as she placed her hand in his. He shook it and grinned down at her. "I'm very pleased to meet you. Finally."

She laughed. "You are such a crazy, crazy man, Michael."

Michael laughed with her and pulled her into his arms to kiss her. He felt her arms around him as she kissed him back. She was home for good this time. Not even death would part them.

When they drew breath, Michael swung her around and lifted her above him joyously. She threw back her head and spread her arms wide to embrace the sky, tears of celebration streaming down her cheeks.

Michael had once read to her how God had cast a man and woman out of Paradise. Yet, for all their human faults and failures, God had shown them the way back in.

The dictionary defines *redemption* as "the action of regaining or gaining possession of something in exchange for payment, or clearing a debt."[9]

Michael redeemed Angel from the Pair-a-Dice brothel, but Jesus redeemed Angel from sin. Michael paid the debt with gold dust; Jesus paid it with His lifeblood.

But there is another act of redemption in this story: Michael and Angel redeemed their marriage together. Michael regained possession of it by investing hours of prayer; Angel regained it through confession and an unreserved commitment of her heart, mind, and body.

Love redeemed them and their marriage.

The Bible tells of another redemption story in Genesis 22:

> Some time later, God tested Abraham's faith. "Abraham!" God called.
>
> "Yes," he replied. "Here I am."

"Take your son, your only son—yes, Isaac, whom you love so much—and go to the land of Moriah. Go and sacrifice him as a burnt offering on one of the mountains, which I will show you." (verses 1–2)

Whoa! God wanted a sacrifice. Not a lamb, not a bull, not even Abraham's other son, Ishmael. He wanted Isaac, the son of promise, Sarah's son, the son Abraham and Sarah spent years waiting for. God wanted Abraham to sacrifice the person he loved best, just as God wanted Michael to let Angel go that last time, knowing she would need the freedom to make her own choice.

Did Abraham try to convince God to sacrifice something else? No. Did he complain? No. Did he question God's sanity? No. He believed, full of faith, that God is trustworthy, even though he didn't understand why God had asked him to do this thing.

The next morning Abraham got up early. He saddled his donkey and took two of his servants with him, along with his son, Isaac. Then he chopped wood for a fire for a burnt offering and set out for the place God had told him about. On the third day of their journey, Abraham looked up and saw the place in the distance. "Stay here with the donkey," Abraham told the servants. "The boy and I will travel a little farther. We will worship there, and then we will come right back."

So Abraham placed the wood for the burnt offering on Isaac's shoulders, while he himself carried the fire and the knife. As the two of them walked on together, Isaac turned to Abraham and said, "Father?"

"Yes, my son?" Abraham replied.

"We have the fire and the wood," the boy said, "but where is the sheep for the burnt offering?"

"God will provide a sheep for the burnt offering, my son," Abraham answered. And they both walked on together.
(verses 3–8)

Did Abraham try to delay? No, he got up early and left with Isaac and a couple of servants. He probably did not mention his purpose to Sarah because her protestations might have weakened his resolve. He took wood and other supplies for the journey. And they began to walk. They walked for three days, a long time to think about what you're about to do. Did he doubt God's goodness on the journey? Did he have second thoughts? Apparently not, because when Isaac asked about the lamb for the altar, Abraham spoke with quiet confidence: "God will provide a sheep for the burnt offering, my son." And he told his servants, "We will come right back."

We. Both of us.

Abraham built the altar of wood and stones. Perhaps tears flowed over his lined cheeks as he and his son arranged the rocks and then piled wood on the altar. When they finished, Abraham may have said to Isaac, his beloved son, his mother's joy, the seed that was to result in many descendants, "My son, you are the lamb God has provided."

And Isaac, dutiful son that he was, allowed his father to bind his hands and feet and lay him on the altar. He was willing, not rebellious, because Isaac also believed in obeying God. When Isaac was in place, with trembling hands Abraham picked up his knife, looked to the heavens, and prepared to cut his son's throat . . . but the Angel of the Lord spoke and halted the proceeding.

"Abraham! Abraham!"

"Yes," Abraham replied. "Here I am!"

"Don't lay a hand on the boy!" the angel said. "Do not hurt him in any way, for now I know that you truly fear God. You have not withheld from me even your son, your only son." (verses 11–12)

The Angel of the Lord was not just any angel. Most theologians believe He was the preincarnate Christ. He was always addressed as God and referred to Himself as God.

Then Abraham looked up and saw a ram caught by its horns in a thicket. So he took the ram and sacrificed it as a burnt offering in place of his son. Abraham named the place Yahweh-Yireh (which means "the LORD will provide"). To this day, people still use that name as a proverb: "On the mountain of the LORD it will be provided." (verses 13–14)

Jesus, who would one day allow Himself to be sacrificed for humankind, provided a substitute for Abraham's precious son.

TO THINK ABOUT

1. Why did God command Abraham to sacrifice his son? Scripture says that God tested Abraham, but God didn't need to know how strong Abraham's faith was. God is all-knowing, so He already knew the strength of Abraham's faith. Maybe God wanted *Abraham* to know how much faith he had. Or perhaps the lesson was intended for Isaac, the willing sacrifice.

Matthew Henry said Abraham's example "is a lively representation . . . of the love of God to us, in delivering up his only-begotten Son to suffer and die for us, as a sacrifice."[10]

On the mountain that day, God redeemed Isaac with a ram. The command was obeyed, the sacrifice made, and the redemption price paid. Thousands of years later, on a hill outside Jerusalem, another command was obeyed, another sacrifice made—and the redemption price for humankind paid.

Have you ever felt God asking you to sacrifice something? What was it? Why do you think He asked this of you?

2. As Angel walked toward Michael, the gray in his hair and the lines on his face became apparent. "Oh, what had she done to him in denying her love, in turning away? She had played God and done what she thought best for him, and all she had done was cause him pain."

The story of Angel and Michael is also the story of every human and Jesus. Have you ever considered how our sin—our refusal to love and obey Him—causes Him pain? How long He has waited for us to leave our sin and accept His love?

Angel wanted to be clean, to be new, for Michael. She wanted to please him. She planned to dedicate the rest of her life to doing that.

How do her thoughts reflect how we should feel about showing our love and unending gratitude to our Savior?

In what other ways do Angel's thoughts and feelings in this last scene reflect our approach to the Lord? Does anything stand between you and the Lord? Is there anything you need to "shed" as you come to Him?

3. If we accept the redemption of Christ, is there any sin we can commit for which we cannot be forgiven?

> O Israel, hope in the LORD;
> for with the LORD there is unfailing love.
> His redemption overflows.
> He himself will redeem Israel
> from every kind of sin. (Psalm 130:7–8)

4. When death, the great equalizer, comes for those who do not know Christ, is there anything they can do to free themselves from its grasp? Is there any amount they can pay for the forgiveness of sin? Is there any payment they can make that is great enough to buy entrance into heaven?

> Why should I fear when trouble comes,
> when enemies surround me?
> They trust in their wealth
> and boast of great riches.

Yet they cannot redeem themselves from death
    by paying a ransom to God.
Redemption does not come so easily,
    for no one can ever pay enough
to live forever
    and never see the grave. (49:5–9)

5. The book of Job contains one of the oldest stories in the Bible, with Job living before Moses. Yet Job had faith in the coming Redeemer promised by God. Not only did Job believe he would be redeemed, but he also believed in the afterlife and that the Redeemer would walk on the earth. You may recognize this beautiful passage on which part of Handel's *Messiah* is based:

As for me, I know that my Redeemer lives,
    and he will stand upon the earth at last.
And after my body has decayed,
    yet in my body I will see God!
I will see him for myself.
    Yes, I will see him with my own eyes.
    I am overwhelmed at the thought! (Job 19:25–27)

You and I have never seen our Redeemer, but one day we will. When we die, our souls will immediately be in God's presence, and when Christ returns, our bodies will be resurrected as supernatural bodies. We will stand before His presence in incorruptible flesh! How does this truth make you feel? Job was overwhelmed; we can be overwhelmed and *grateful,* knowing what Jesus endured to redeem our lives from sin.

On what sure foundation can you build the rest of your life?

Holy, holy, is what the angels sing,
And I expect to help them make the courts of heaven ring;
But when I sing redemption's story, they will fold their
   wings,
For angels never felt the joys that our salvation brings.[11]

Five

THE BRIDE

Rick and I celebrated our golden wedding anniversary on December 21, 2019. The two of us often look at each other and wonder aloud, "How has that much time passed so quickly?"

I still remember our wedding day, which was full of excitement and anxiety. Who in her right mind plans a Christmas wedding? Well, that evening was the only time the church was available. We were expecting one hundred close relatives and friends, and some people were coming a considerable distance and needed lodging. Winter rains were forecasted. Serving in the Marine Corps at El Toro, a ten-hour drive away, Rick had not been in on all the preparations. All he had to do was show up, but that was proving a challenge. A marine serves at the pleasure of the Corps, and one commanding officer thought it funny to refuse permission for leave to get married. Rick told me he'd go AWOL if necessary. And then what? Spend our honeymoon in the brig?

Those weren't the only reasons I had bridal jitters. I peered down the aisle to make sure Rick stood at the front, and then I clung to my father's arm as he walked me down the aisle. What if Rick changed his mind? It happens. What if he decided I wasn't good enough for him and he'd rather wait for someone better to come along? I'd heard stories of brides left at the altar. In fact, the night before, I'd attended the wedding of a dear friend who wept buckets before the ceremony because she knew she shouldn't marry the man waiting for her at the end of the aisle. Would Rick have second or third thoughts and decide to call the whole thing off? Burdened by guilt over mistakes I'd made, all of which made me feel unworthy to be his wife, I would have been broken and crushed, but I wouldn't have blamed him.

I felt a mingling of surprised relief and joy when Rick remained at the front of the church, looking straight at me, waiting. We'd known each other since fifth grade, but we'd both been through a lot in the intervening years. Life had battered and bruised both of us in different ways. Neither of us knew the full extent of the damage or what we were getting in a spouse.

All the details of the perfect wedding were there: the cream-white dress and veil denoting purity, the celebratory mood of family and friends who were filling the church to be witnesses. My father gave me away to a young man he barely knew, trusting that my love was the only necessary recommendation. After the vows, I had a new name and new identity. I would never again be just me. I would be connected to another human being by law as well as heart and soul.

After the service, the reception confirmed our oneness. We received guests as man and wife. Toasts were made to bless the new couple, a cake was cut and shared, and gifts were stacked high to help set up a new household. Rick and I removed our wedding clothes and donned everyday wear. After being pelted by rice, good wishes, and laughter, we headed off on our honeymoon, where we would become one flesh and begin the journey of what it means to be man and wife, living together with an intimacy we had not previously shared.

Oh, how romantic. Yes. But it isn't long before the differences between two melded people show up. One is thrifty; the other, spendthrift. One likes to get from point A to point B directly, while the other wants to meander and stop to take pictures. Two sets of parents want the couple to be at *their* house for Thanksgiving and Christmas and New Year's and Easter and every family birthday. Friends still want time, especially the single ones who don't have to worry about pleasing a spouse. Hidden addictions rear their ugly heads. One person wants the house spotless; the other leaves dirty laundry on the bathroom floor. One loves animals; the other has allergies.

We waited seven years to have children, then had three in quick succession. Another learning curve was parenthood: joy and fun mingled with trials and tribulations. One parent is a rigid disciplinarian, and the other just wants to be the children's friend.

Rick and I discovered marriage is hard work, but then anything worthwhile is. We did a lot of shouting in the early days and a lot of making up too. We were two strong-willed people, each absolutely convinced his or her way was right. Bar the gates! Man the cannons!

We came near to divorce several times. We were both stubborn and miserable, each thinking the other was to blame and should change. I was learning, finally, that I couldn't change anyone. I couldn't even change myself. That's when I became willing to try anything, even God, to stop the pain and anger. Pain is what brings us to our knees.

God listens to His wandering, bleating sheep, and He knew when this bride was ready to listen and learn.

Obey. Submit. Incendiary words in our culture that puts individuality and independence on the throne. Especially when I'd had *obey* deleted from the traditional wedding ceremony. I was all for women's liberation. *Obey* was a four-letter word.

Little did I know, *submission* is far from a dirty word. It's an amazing, God-designed concept that brings people closer. Submit to God. Submit to one another. Jesus is the prime example of submission's cost and the beauty it brings. It distinguishes our separate roles in a relationship and what we are each called to do. It's a loving acknowledgment of our value as individual human beings. When love is at the center of submission, it brings about a humble, mutually beneficial cooperation between two people that builds both up and makes them into a whole as well.

Those God-designed concepts were evident in our wedding ceremony. They point to what it takes, through faith and obedience to God, to make a wonderful marriage. When one begins to change, the dynamics of a relationship change as well. Each of us became new individual creations in Christ, bound together in marriage, with unique purposes both individually and as a couple. A new Spirit inhabited each of us and our relationship. Differences and trials still come—and always will—but we stick close to God and work and walk through them together.

We struggled mightily against each other for years. When we gave up and sought God, everything changed. We started our mornings together, a time that remains precious. We fanned each other's dreams and helped each other step out in faith and take risks to achieve them.

Our children observed our before-and-after-Jesus marriage. I'll never forget the day our daughter said, "You and Daddy have such a strong relationship." She was in a school where every other child in her class came from a broken or blended home.

Our marriage had been broken too, but God mended us. Miraculous turnarounds happen when we kneel before God. Our marriage has stood as a rare example of what can happen when people surrender to the Lord and live victoriously.

STUDY 5.1

Married Without Love

A loveless marriage is a contradiction in terms.
WILLIAM BARCLAY, SCOTTISH THEOLOGIAN

SOMEONE TOOK ANGEL'S *hand. She thought it was Lucky at first, but Lucky's hand was soft and small. This one was large and hard, the skin rough with calluses. "Just say yes."*

She would agree to wed Satan himself if it would get her out of the Palace. "Why not?" she managed.

She drifted on a sea of pain and quiet voices. The room was full of them. Lucky was there, and Doc, and the other man whose voice was so familiar, but she still couldn't place it. She felt someone slip a ring on her finger. Her head was raised gently, and she was given something bitter to drink.

Lucky took her hand. "They're rigging his wagon so he can take you home with him. You'll sleep all the way with the laudanum you drank. You won't feel nothing." She felt Lucky touch her hair. "You're a regular married lady now, Angel. He had a wedding ring on a chain around his neck. He said it belonged to his mother. His mother, Angel. He put his mother's wedding ring on your finger. Can you hear me, honey?"

Angel wanted to ask who she had married, but what did it matter? The pain gradually receded. She was so tired. Maybe she would die after all. It would all be over then.

A friend recently told me she'd read a book on psychological trauma and that the book described Angel perfectly.

When I began to write *Redeeming Love,* I never researched using any books about trauma or psychology. I just opened my Bible, sat at my computer, and prayed, and God showed me Angel's life, inside and out. I never experienced the things she did, but I *felt* all the things she felt. I identified with Angel in the way I kept turning away from God.

On a bulletin board in front of me, I pinned a couple of pictures from a women's magazine. The images showed a little girl who'd been kidnapped around the age of eight, then spotted—terrified—in a porn film. A few years later, she "performed" in another film. Around twelve, she looked old, worn. That broke my heart. I'd look at those pictures and think, *I'm writing this for her.*

Since writing *Redeeming Love,* I've received letters from women and men who have been through devastating experiences as children and adults. They survived incest and trafficking, prostitution, exotic dancing, imprisonment, being battered victims . . .

The kind of exploitation prevalent in their lives damages the soul and puts up walls, so the victims find it hard to understand the love of God. The abuse also provides an excuse to reject the Lord's salvation: *God could never love someone like me.* So many victims are conditioned to expect and accept abuse. In *Redeeming Love,* I tried to show the sort of codependence that often develops between the abused and abuser, a strange pairing that occurs over and over to the destruction of both.

One of the things I hope you take away from this study is the desire to examine your choices. Are they healthy and not based solely on need or the fear of being alone? A large part of being able to make wise choices is knowing who you are in Christ, knowing the value God places on you as an individual. *You are worth the life-blood of His beloved Son.*

We are so precious in God's sight. He longs for a relationship with each of us. If we don't fully understand that, we can slip into relationships that reflect how we feel about ourselves. Those relationships are never God's best for us.

I hope you will see yourself through God's eyes. Once you become whole in Christ by putting your faith in Him, you can recognize the unwholesome relationships you've had in the past. You will notice when you're tempted to fall into the same kind of relationship again, and you will know to run from it.

God wants you to experience love that is true, honest, patient, kind, and unselfish. He wants you to find love that "bears all things, believes all things, hopes all things, endures all things" (1 Corinthians 13:7, NASB). He wants you to be able to stand unashamed before your life partner.

He sees you as you are, and still He draws you "with bonds of love" (Hosea 11:4, NASB).

THE STORY BEHIND THE STORY

As I mentioned before, *Redeeming Love* is a fictional exploration of the true story told in the biblical book of Hosea. Hosea was a prophet of God during the time when Israel was a divided country. He operated in the northern kingdom, the nation known as Israel. (The southern kingdom was known as Judah. Jerusalem, home to the holy temple, was located in the southern kingdom.)

Hosea didn't set out to be a prophet. It's not the sort of occupation a child aspires to, because the calling has to come from God.

Hosea could have been a farmer like most men of that time, but one day he heard the voice of God. God had a message for Hosea, but it was uniquely personal and more than a little odd. The Lord told him to take a wife—and not just any woman would do. Hosea was to marry a prostitute.

> When the LORD first began speaking to Israel through Hosea, he said to him, "Go and marry a prostitute, so that some of her children will be conceived in prostitution. This will illustrate how Israel has acted like a prostitute by turning against the LORD and worshiping other gods."
>
> So Hosea married Gomer, the daughter of Diblaim, and she became pregnant and gave Hosea a son. (Hosea 1:2–3)

Where did Hosea find his wife? He didn't have to visit the urban red-light district or a brothel. In those days, many of the people of Israel had fallen away from God, especially in the north. After King Solomon died, his heir, Rehoboam, planned to increase the people's taxes and enraged them to the point that the northern half of the kingdom rebelled and walked away from him. Jeroboam became king of the northern kingdom. Because he had no holy temple where his people could worship, he established sacred high places, installed goat and calf idols, and appointed his own priests. The priests who remained loyal to God moved south, unable to tolerate the idolatry around them (2 Chronicles 10:12–11:16).

As years passed and kings came and went, the worship of Baal crept back into the kingdom of Israel. Baal was a chief deity of Canaan, the god of life and fertility, war, and whatever else the people wanted him to be. From his name we get *Beelzebub*, another name for Satan. The name fits because Baal worship replaced the rightful worship of Adonai.

When the children of Israel first entered the land of Canaan, God commanded them to conquer the land and rid it entirely of the Canaanites (Deuteronomy 7:1–2). The children of Israel, however, began to believe the Canaanite communities were no threat. So, in disobedience to God's command, they allowed pagan communities to remain. Once the pagan and Hebrew people intermingled, the Canaanite religion appealed to the Hebrews and many of them adopted Baal worship.

The worship of Baal enticed the children of Israel for several reasons. First, most of the people were farmers, and Baal was the god of fertility and agriculture. Several rituals associated with Baal worship had to do with seasonal cycles. In the spring, sacrifices of food, drink, and animals were made to entreat the rains to water the earth, ensuring a good crop. Worshippers engaged in sex with male and female "sacred" prostitutes, usually in small rooms behind the statue of the god, believing that these acts would ensure fruitfulness and productivity.

The immorality of Baal worship also appealed to the people of Israel, for the practice gave them a socially acceptable reason to indulge the desires of their flesh. They lost their regard for marriage as a sacred commitment and set aside the worship of Yahweh, along with adherence to His laws.

Baal worship led the people of Israel to adopt a casual approach to God. Their Canaanite neighbors were polytheistic, worshipping many gods. The Hebrews thought they could worship Baal *and* Adonai—and any other god they chose. The Canaanites must have seemed more sophisticated and free spirited, having knowledge of and freedom to worship many gods, all of whom granted more personal liberty—a license to sin—than the God who had brought them out of Egypt.

When Hosea went searching for a wife, he didn't have to go far. He simply went to the nearest temple of Baal, where he could take his pick from the many prostitutes. He chose a woman called Gomer.

Scripture tells us Gomer was the daughter of Diblaim, a man we know nothing about. Some have suggested that "daughter of

Diblaim" might mean she was from the Moabite town of Dibla-tayim, but it is far more likely she was simply Diblaim's daughter. She was probably Jewish but did not worship Adonai. She likely had grown up with her parents and, as soon as she was sexually mature, been taken to work at one of the temples as a professional prosti-tute. She was probably twelve or thirteen at the time.

Some scholars believe Gomer could not have been a prostitute when Hosea married her because God would never tell a prophet to marry such a woman. Such thinking, however, not only contradicts the scripture but also supposes that a holy man would never associ-ate with sinners. But isn't that what Jesus did? He ate and drank with sinners and tax collectors. He came to reach those who needed a savior, not those who were satisfied with their religious status.

The Bible gives us no details about what Gomer thought when Hosea came to her with an offer of marriage. She willingly chose marriage, though, because she had to choose to leave the service of Baal. Perhaps she had grown tired of her life as a prostitute. Perhaps she felt neglected, lonely, and unloved. She might have been left at the temple because her parents could not afford to feed her or per-haps because they wanted to raise sons, not daughters. Since God warned Hosea that "some of her children" would be conceived in prostitution, she may have been pregnant when Hosea asked her to marry him.

In any case, Hosea went to the temple and asked Gomer to leave with him and become his wife. She might have laughed in his face. Why had a farmer-prophet, one of the few remaining worshippers of Adonai in the northern kingdom, ventured inside a pagan tem-ple? Why was he speaking to her? Most righteous Hebrews avoided her whenever she wandered about the city. Some people spat on her. Most men, especially those who had been intimate with her at the temple, refused to make eye contact.

But Hosea—young, sincere, and devout—stood in front of her. Imagine how it might have happened. "Adonai has spoken to me," he declared. "He said I am to marry a prostitute and have children with her. I will marry you if you are willing."

Not the most romantic proposal, but Gomer might not have had many offers. Most sacred prostitutes remained at the temple all their lives, and men regarded them as little more than warm sacks of skin.

As far as we know, Gomer didn't know Hosea—didn't know where he lived, whether he was rich or poor, brilliant or dull. But he likely had a determined look in his eyes, and she had grown weary of her life in the temple. After considering her alternatives—there weren't many—she said, "Yes, I will marry you."

Hosea took his new wife to his home, made her comfortable, and introduced her to his neighbors. They must have looked at Gomer in surprise, then wished Hosea well and hurried back into their houses. Sure, Hosea was a prophet and claimed that God had told him to marry a prostitute. But surely Hosea had misunderstood. No holy God would do such a thing.

They shook their heads and lowered the leather shades on their windows. They had no interest in knowing anything more about the house next door.

Hosea loved Gomer faithfully, as a godly man should love his wife, and Gomer became pregnant. When their baby boy was born, Adonai spoke to Hosea again: "Name the child Jezreel, for I am about to punish King Jehu's dynasty to avenge the murders he committed at Jezreel. In fact, I will bring an end to Israel's independence. I will break its military power in the Jezreel Valley" (Hosea 1:4–5).

The name *Jezreel* means "God will scatter." God was telling Hosea—and all Israel—that He would punish them for going after other gods. They had been unfaithful to Him, and they would be scattered as a result.

David Guzik, a pastor, explained that *Jezreel* also refers to the valley of Jezreel, where Jehu killed all the descendants of Ahab and established his throne (2 Kings 10:11). Guzik wrote, "God directed Hosea to name his son Jezreel to confirm His promise to avenge the bloodshed of Jezreel by judging the house of Jehu."[12]

Then Gomer conceived again and gave birth to a daughter. And God told Hosea, "Name your daughter Lo-ruhamah—'Not loved'—for I will no longer show love to the people of Israel or forgive them. But I will show love to the people of Judah. I will free them from their enemies—not with weapons and armies or horses and charioteers, but by my power as the LORD their God" (Hosea 1:6–7).

The name *Lo-ruhamah* means "no mercy." Every time Gomer called her daughter, she would remind anyone listening of the coming judgment.

God did show mercy to Judah, for the army of Assyria, which had earlier destroyed Israel, attacked Judah but did not conquer them. Guzik noted, "God miraculously fought on behalf of Judah against Assyria when the angel of the Lord killed 185,000 Assyrian soldiers in one night (2 Kings 19:35)."[13]

While Judah and her kings were more faithful to the Lord, it doesn't matter if Judah was more worthy, because all mercy is undeserved. Guzik wrote, "If one *deserves* leniency, then leniency is a matter of justice, not mercy. Mercy is only shown to the *guilty*. Therefore, it is within the wise and loving heart of God to show mercy to whom He will show mercy (Romans 9:15)."[14]

After Gomer weaned Lo-ruhamah, she bore another son. Then God said, "Name him Lo-ammi—'Not my people'—for Israel is not my people, and I am not their God" (Hosea 1:9). Every time Gomer and Hosea spoke their younger son's name, they would remember that the people of Israel had chosen Baal over Adonai.

This child may also have reminded Hosea of something else—Gomer may have gone back to the temple of Baal before Lo-ammi's birth, so it was possible that her third baby was not Hosea's son. If the boy looked nothing like Hosea or his older brother and sister,

Hosea would have felt a pang of grief every time he looked at his youngest child, a painful reminder of Gomer's unfaithfulness.

TO THINK ABOUT

1. How is our self-image reflected in the things we do? When we are feeling good about ourselves, what kind of clothing do we select? When we are feeling dumpy and ugly and bloated, what kind of clothing do we select?

How is our self-image reflected in our friends? Our friends are often a mirror in which we see ourselves. What do your friends reveal about what you think of yourself?

How is our self-worth reflected in the men we date or once dated? What have your choices said about your self-image?

If Jesus loves us enough to have given His life for us and cares enough to sit at the Father's right hand and pray for us daily (Mark 16:19; Hebrews 7:25), how should we view ourselves now? We are to be humble, yes, but we are daughters of the King of the universe! We are loved and cherished. So, what is the proper basis for our self-worth?

2. When the children of Israel first entered Canaan, their promised land, God told them to cleanse it of all the inhabitants. To the modern reader, this seems cruel and unmerciful. Why would God command such a thing? Could the Canaanites have been an evil influence on the children of Israel? Is it possible that the Canaanites had earned judgment from God?

Consider this passage, which is part of God's covenant with Abraham, given long before Isaac's birth:

The LORD said to Abram, "You can be sure that your descendants will be strangers in a foreign land, where they will be oppressed as slaves for 400 years. But I will punish the nation that enslaves them, and in the end they will come away with great wealth. (As for you, you will die in peace and be buried at a ripe old age.) After four generations your descendants will return here to this land, *for the sins of the Amorites do not yet warrant their destruction.*" (Genesis 15:13–16, emphasis added)

Do you see? God gave the Amorites (Canaanites) more than four hundred years to repent. Because He is all-knowing and can see the future, He knew they would not turn from their sinful ways. By the time the children of Israel left Egypt, the Canaanites had committed so much evil, generation after generation, that they deserved destruction.

What does this reality tell you about God's patience? What does it reveal about humankind's perspective? What does it say about evil influences in our own lives?

3. Baal worship gave the people everything they wanted: permission to sin under the guise of religious devotion and freedom to worship any gods they pleased. Living in the United States of America, I have seen our society shift from one in which everyone has at least a basic knowledge of and respect for God to one in which He is mocked and believers are considered ignorant, bigoted, and hate filled.

We are not all that different from the northern kingdom of Israel. If God judged the Israelites for their attitudes and actions, will He not judge us as well? Why, or why not?

4. For a moment, place yourself in Gomer's situation. How would you have reacted if a young prophet came to your workplace and asked you to marry him? Would you have accepted? Why, or why not?

5. At God's command, Hosea gave his children names that meant "God will scatter," "no mercy," and "not my people." At the beginning of *Redeeming Love*, Angel would have said those names applied to her. Her loved ones had been scattered, so she was alone. God, she believed, had shown her no mercy. And she never ever would have said she was a child of God.

But by the end of the novel, Angel would no longer have claimed those names. How would she have described herself then?

I have been the LORD your God
ever since I brought you out of Egypt.
You must acknowledge no God but me,
for there is no other savior.
I took care of you in the wilderness,
in that dry and thirsty land.
But when you had eaten and were satisfied,
you became proud and forgot me. (Hosea 13:4–6)

STUDY 5.2

Love Is a Verb

Love is a verb.

STEPHEN R. COVEY, *THE 7 HABITS OF*
HIGHLY EFFECTIVE PEOPLE

ANGEL WANTED TO *resist but was afraid. What was Michael going to do to her now? In this mood, could he be as brutal as Duke? "Why did you come for me?"*

"You're my wife."

"I left the ring on the table! I didn't steal it."

"That didn't change a thing. We're still married."

"You could've just forgotten about it."

He stopped and glared at her. "It's a lifetime commitment in my book, lady. It's not an arrangement you nullify when things get a little tough to bear."

She searched his face in confusion. "Even after you just found me—" He started walking again, pulling her along with him. She didn't understand him. She didn't understand him at all. "Why?"

"Because I love you," he said thickly. He swung her around in front of him, his eyes tormented. "That simple, Amanda. I love you. When are you going to understand what that means?"

⟨≈⟩

E arly in her marriage, Angel found a ride back to Pair-a-Dice with Paul. She discovered the brothel destroyed and resorted to working as a prostitute for the owner of the saloon. Before long, Michael stormed in to take her home. His persistent love bewildered Angel. How could he love her after all she had put him through?

Hosea was in a similar situation with Gomer. She had left him and returned to her former life.

> Then the LORD said to me, "Go and love your wife again, even though she commits adultery with another lover. This will illustrate that the LORD still loves Israel, even though the people have turned to other gods and love to worship them."
>
> So I bought her back for fifteen pieces of silver and five bushels of barley and a measure of wine. Then I said to her, "You must live in my house for many days and stop your prostitution. During this time, you will not have sexual relations with anyone, not even with me."
>
> This shows that Israel will go a long time without a king or prince, and without sacrifices, sacred pillars, priests, or even idols! But afterward the people will return and devote themselves to the LORD their God and to David's descendant, their king. In the last days, they will tremble in awe of the LORD and of his goodness. (Hosea 3)

Some have supposed that Gomer had moved in with another man, but since Hosea had to pay a price to redeem her, it's more likely she had gone back to the temple of Baal. Why would a woman leave a loving husband and children to return to a life of soulless sex? Was she experiencing the same struggles Angel faced? Did she feel defiant? Did she feel unworthy of love? Was she afraid of facing the truth about herself? Was she afraid to hope?

Gomer was in an unusual situation. How would you feel if God told your husband to give your children names that referred to coming judgment, a lack of compassion, and a disowned people?

The second time Hosea took Gomer home, he used a different approach. Instead of showering her with love and compassion, he told her they would live together platonically, as brother and sister. They would tend to their children, and he would be kind, but he would not have sexual relations with her.

Yet he did not stop loving her. "Go and *love your wife* again," the Lord had told him, and Hosea's redemption of Gomer was an act of continuing love. He loved her too much to let her continue in that horrible place. He loved her too much to let her be treated as a sexual commodity. He loved her too much to let her destroy her heart and soul.

He wanted to know her, to be one with her as God had designed, but she was not ready for an honest relationship. So they took a sabbatical from sex.

They took this sabbatical, I believe, for two reasons. First, it was to complete the metaphor. God had been honest with Hosea from the beginning: his marriage to Gomer was to be a living metaphor representing God's relationship with Israel. He loved Israel and chose them from all the nations of the earth, but not because they were intellectual or mighty or numerous.

He explained His reason in Deuteronomy 7:6–9:

> You are a holy people, who belong to the LORD your God. Of all the people on earth, the LORD your God has chosen you to be his own special treasure.
>
> The LORD did not set his heart on you and choose you because you were more numerous than other nations, for you were the smallest of all nations! Rather, it was simply that the

LORD loves you, and he was keeping the oath he had sworn to your ancestors. That is why the LORD rescued you with such a strong hand from your slavery and from the oppressive hand of Pharaoh, king of Egypt. Understand, therefore, that the LORD your God is indeed God. He is the faithful God who keeps his covenant for a thousand generations and lavishes his unfailing love on those who love him and obey his commands.

Of all the nations on earth, God chose Israel. He betrothed Himself to her, and she proved unfaithful to Him, pursuing other gods as an adulteress pursues men. In Hosea and Gomer's marriage, God wanted the people of Israel to see an image of what they had done, a flesh-and-blood representation of their relationship. And Hosea 3:4–5 tells us that this sabbatical symbolized a coming time in which Israel would be without a king and without religious observances—a time that would end when the people retuned and devoted themselves to God.

The second reason they took this sabbatical had to do with attitude adjustment. Surely Gomer needed time to change her thoughts about sex. It was not meant to be a mindless, meaningless act between a prostitute and a customer, nor was it meant as an act to pacify the pagan god of fertility. She had come into her marriage with her past as close as a shadow and had not taken time to reflect and adjust her attitude about the act of marriage. She had conceived her first child soon after her marriage, and a second child quickly after the first. Gomer needed time to put her past to death. She needed to learn why God had instituted sex as a loving act within marriage.

Hosea also needed time to reflect and adjust his attitude. He had been a loving husband from the beginning, but perhaps he expected too much from Gomer. A time of restraint would be good for both of them.

Yet the time of being together but apart would come to an end—in both the metaphorical and the physical senses.

God said,

"Then I will win her back once again.
   I will lead her into the desert
   and speak tenderly to her there.
I will return her vineyards to her
   and transform the Valley of Trouble into a gateway of hope.
She will give herself to me there,
   as she did long ago when she was young,
   when I freed her from her captivity in Egypt.
When that day comes," says the LORD,
   "you will call me 'my husband'
   instead of 'my master.'
O Israel, I will wipe the many names of Baal from your lips,
   and you will never mention them again."
   (Hosea 2:14–17)

Notice that God said, "I will *win* her back once again." He would not drive her, drag her, or force her. He would woo and win her with love, for the power of His love is irresistible. Evil had captured Israel and held her captive, burdening her with the heavy chains of falsehood, fear, and shame, but God would show her that He is trustworthy and loving. Why should they look to Baal for provision and plentiful harvests when God was the one who brought the sun and rain? Why did they seek the immorality of the temple prostitutes when God had designed marriage as a relationship that could offer far more than a casual fling?

Once Israel listened to God, she would repent of her sin and yield herself again to Him. And when that day arrived, she would never again speak of Baal but would refer to God as "my husband."

"I will make you my wife forever,
   showing you righteousness and justice,
   unfailing love and compassion.

I will be faithful to you and make you mine,
    and you will finally know me as the LORD.

"In that day, I will answer,"
    says the LORD.
"I will answer the sky as it pleads for clouds.
    And the sky will answer the earth with rain.
Then the earth will answer the thirsty cries
    of the grain, the grapevines, and the olive trees.
And they in turn will answer,
    'Jezreel'—'God plants!'
At that time I will plant a crop of Israelites
    and raise them for myself.
I will show love
    to those I called 'Not loved.'
And to those I called 'Not my people,'
    I will say, 'Now you are my people.'
And they will reply, 'You are our God!'" (verses 19–23)

Not only would Israel be reunited with God, but Gomer and Hosea would also experience a new beginning in their marriage. When the time was right, when Hosea could see that Gomer was willing to set the past aside and be loved, he wooed and won her. She came alive in the marriage, fully participating for the first time with her husband and children.

This was a new beginning for their children too. *Jezreel* came to mean "God plants," and their daughter received a name that means "loved"! The third child's name would now mean "you are mine," for Hosea would be his father, whether or not the boy was his biological offspring.

Why did Israel go astray?

"O Israel and Judah,
    what should I do with you?" asks the LORD.

"For your love vanishes like the morning mist
    and disappears like dew in the sunlight." (6:4)

The Israelites' love for God had been like the morning dew, vanishing the moment the sun began to shine. They were infatuated with God, loving Him for a moment, and then they forgot Him when other pleasures beckoned.

Jesus told a story with similar meaning:

"Listen! A farmer went out to plant some seed. As he scattered it across his field, some of the seed fell on a footpath, and the birds came and ate it. Other seed fell on shallow soil with underlying rock. The seed sprouted quickly because the soil was shallow. But the plant soon wilted under the hot sun, and since it didn't have deep roots, it died. Other seed fell among thorns that grew up and choked out the tender plants so they produced no grain. Still other seeds fell on fertile soil, and they sprouted, grew, and produced a crop that was thirty, sixty, and even a hundred times as much as had been planted!" Then he said, "Anyone with ears to hear should listen and understand." (Mark 4:3–9)

The first seeds in Jesus's parable represent those who hear the truth about God and quickly reject it. The second group comprises those who initially receive God's truth with joy but who fall away as soon as they face hardship. The pressures of the world arise and choke out God's message in the hearts of the third group. But the fourth group of seeds sprouts, takes root, grows, and bears fruit (verses 14–20). These are the ones who withstand the heat of the sun, persist among the weeds, and find their purpose bearing fruit.

TO THINK ABOUT

1. The children of Israel were not bearing fruit. God intended them to be a blessing to the world, showing His power and glory to all the nations, and they failed miserably. But God did not give up on them, and He will not give up on you.

Have you experienced a time when you fell away from God? What brought you back to Him?

2. Another reason Israel strayed from God is found in Hosea 7:1–2:

> I want to heal Israel, but its sins are too great.
> Samaria is filled with liars.
> Thieves are on the inside
> and bandits on the outside!
> Its people don't realize
> that I am watching them.
> Their sinful deeds are all around them,
> and I see them all.

The people of Israel forgot that God is omnipresent and omniscient. He is everywhere and knew everything they had done. He is El Roi, the God who sees, and He saw all their sin.

We cannot escape God's eyes. We may be able to hide things from our acquaintances, our closest friends, and even our families, but we cannot hide anything from God. He knows our deeds and thoughts. He reads the secret emotions roiling in our treacherous hearts. He knows our weaknesses and our fears, and He knows the lies we tell ourselves to justify our actions.

God is never deceived. He knows all.

Have you ever nursed a secret sin? Why did it appeal to you?

Did the Holy Spirit convict you of it? Did you repent and confess it? How did it feel to be forgiven of that sin?

3. There is good news: God is willing to forgive our sins when we repent and turn from them. When we come back to Him, He forgives and does not hold our sins against us.

> "The day is coming," says the LORD, "when I will make a new covenant with the people of Israel and Judah. This covenant will not be like the one I made with their ancestors when I took them by the hand and brought them out of the land of Egypt. They broke that covenant, though I loved them as a husband loves his wife," says the LORD.
>
> "But this is the new covenant I will make with the people of Israel after those days," says the LORD. "I will put my instructions deep within them, and I will write them on their hearts. I will be their God, and they will be my people." (Jeremiah 31:31–33)

How do you think Gomer and Hosea felt when their marriage had been renewed and the past forgiven? How did their renewed marriage benefit their children? Their friends and neighbors?

4. God loves us. It's that simple. But so many people don't understand what God's love is all about.

God loved Israel. Hosea loved Gomer with that same kind of love—love that sacrifices and keeps its word. As Michael said, it's a lifetime commitment.

Do you remember the overwhelming rush of love you felt when you got your first pet? At your wedding? When you held your first baby? Love is a powerful feeling, yes, but it's also a powerful commitment. At least it should be.

How do we show God we love Him? Jesus said, "If you love me, obey my commandments" (John 14:15). Emotion is one thing; love in action is quite another. God knows everything, so He knows the feelings in your heart. How can you put your faith into action to show Him—which shows the world—how much you love Him?

5. The emotional rush of love is enough to make a grown man giddy. But the emotional commitment of love is enough to make a grown man surrender his life.

Who has loved you enough to sacrifice for you? When you were young, did your parents sacrifice their hard-earned money to provide you with piano lessons? Tutoring? Designer tennis shoes? Did your mother stay up late helping you with projects? Did your father spend hours on the bleachers watching you play a sport? Or vice versa?

Whom do you love enough to sacrifice for? Why do you love them? What would you do to prove your love for them?

Love is one of God's greatest gifts to us, and it is part of His character. Can you imagine living in a world where love did not exist? I can't. It was love that drove God to create the universe in the first place. He longed for beings with whom He could share creation and have intimate relationships.

Take time today to write a letter to God, thanking Him for loving you and blessing you with people to love.

When Israel was a child, I loved him,
*   and I called my son out of Egypt.*
But the more I called to him,
*   the farther he moved from me,*
offering sacrifices to the images of Baal
*   and burning incense to idols.*

I myself taught Israel how to walk,
    leading him along by the hand.
But he doesn't know or even care
    that it was I who took care of him.
I led Israel along
    with my ropes of kindness and love. (Hosea 11:1–4)

The Bride's Purpose

*There are two great days in a person's life: the day we are
born and the day we discover why.*

AUTHOR UNKNOWN

EVERYTHING MICHAEL DID *had purpose. Angel thought of her
own life and how meaningless and miserable it had been before him.
Her very reason to be alive now depended on him. And Michael depended on the earth, the rains, the warmth of the sun. And his God.*

Especially his God.

I'd be dead by now if Michael hadn't come back for me. I'd be
rotting in a shallow, unmarked grave.

*She was consumed with gratitude and filled with an aching hu-
mility that this man loved her. Why, of all the other women of the
world, had he chosen her? She was so undeserving. It was inconceiv-
able.*

Michael had found his purpose in life. At this point in the
novel, Angel was still searching.

Why did God create us? Why are any of us alive? Are we mere

animals, born by chance? Or does God really have a unique purpose for each of us?

I used to believe the purpose of life was to find happiness. I don't believe that anymore. I believe we are all given gifts from our Father and that our purpose is to offer them to Him. He knows how He wants us to use them. I used to struggle to find happiness. I used to work hard to attain it. By the world's standards, I was successful. But it was all meaningless vanity.

Now I have joy. I have everything I ever dreamed of having: a love that is so precious I can find no words to describe it. I haven't achieved this through my own efforts. I certainly haven't done anything to earn it or even deserve it. I have received it as a free gift from the Lord, the everlasting God.

Before the world began, before God created the earth or the first man and woman, God existed with the Son and the Holy Spirit.

"Father," Jesus prayed on the night He was betrayed, "I want these whom you have given me to be with me where I am. Then they can see all the glory you gave me because you loved me even before the world began!" (John 17:24).

Unity and love existed among the Godhead, and God had no need to create a world for humankind. But He did. Why? Men and women have been asking themselves for generations, *Why do I exist? What is my purpose in life? Why am I here?*

You are here—you exist—to glorify your Creator.

> Bring all who claim me as their God,
>> for I have made them for my glory.
>> It was I who created them. (Isaiah 43:7)

Those who believe are united with Christ and have received an inheritance from God. He chose us before we were born, and "he makes everything work out according to his plan" (Ephesians 1:11).

There is no longer Jew or Gentile, slave or free, male and female. For you are all one in Christ Jesus. (Galatians 3:28)

In this new life, it doesn't matter if you are a Jew or a Gentile,
circumcised or uncircumcised, barbaric, uncivilized, slave, or
free. Christ is all that matters, and he lives in all of us. (Colos-
sians 3:11)

Knowing that God created us to glorify Him means *we are important to Him.* We have a God-centered purpose.

But wait, you may be thinking. *What about me? What about my
dreams and goals?*

This is a beautiful thing about God's plan. God's intent for you
to glorify Him does not neglect you at all. God created you to glorify Him *as you live* the abundant, meaningful, significant life He
designed uniquely for you.

Jesus said, "The thief's purpose is to steal and kill and destroy.
My purpose is to give them a rich and satisfying life" (John 10:10).

Asaph, one of the psalmists, wrote,

Whom have I in heaven but you?
    I desire you more than anything on earth.
My health may fail, and my spirit may grow weak,
    but God remains the strength of my heart;
    he is mine forever. (Psalm 73:25–26)

You might think it sounds selfish for God to want glory for
Himself, but that is a strictly human point of view. It *is* wrong for
humans to want glory for themselves. When we crave glory, we steal
it from God, who ultimately deserves it. But if God desires glory,
from whom is He stealing it?[15] No one. A soldier who saves his pla-
toon on the field of battle may win glory and honor, but wasn't it
God who kept him safe and gave him the strength to perform his
daring deed? A soloist who sings a magnificent song deserves praise

for her hard practice, but wasn't it God who gave her a unique voice? Everything praiseworthy in a person comes from God. In heaven,

> whenever the living beings give glory and honor and thanks to the one sitting on the throne (the one who lives forever and ever), the twenty-four elders fall down and worship the one sitting on the throne (the one who lives forever and ever). And they lay their crowns before the throne and say,
> "You are worthy, O Lord our God,
>> to receive glory and honor and power.
> For you created all things,
>> and they exist because you created what you pleased."
> (Revelation 4:9–11)

God is the creator, and nothing would exist if He had not created it. No one would exist without Him. No virtues—honor, courage, truth, moral strength—would exist without Him, for they exude from His nature. The evils of the world—cowardice, falsehood, moral weakness—result when God's nature is removed from a situation. Evil is the absence of goodness. Darkness is the absence of light.

These are profound thoughts—easy to read, harder to digest. The world around us would like to forget God entirely, attributing our existence to evolution, our goodness to humanism, and our achievements to human intellect. People prefer to believe that humankind is getting better, stronger, and more virtuous, but all we have to do is look around to realize the opposite is true. Government without God's influence becomes corrupt. Education without acknowledging God becomes foolishness. Society without God's moral guidelines becomes lawless and flagrantly immoral.

The northern kingdom of Israel had pagan temples with sacred prostitutes, but modern nations have sex trafficking and legalized prostitution. We also have idolatry, both subtle and overt. I have been in shops that sell statues of saints that supposedly grant your request if you repeat a prayer (an incantation) and bury the statue in the ground. How is that different from idol worship? You are not trusting in God; you are trusting in the statue or candle or whatever.

Modern people commit the same sins as the Israelites of old, and we justify our sins in the same way. But God's forgiveness is unchanging and just as available today as it was in Hosea's era.

God created us in His image. What does that mean? It does *not* mean we look like Him physically, for God is a spirit, and a spirit does not have a body. We are created in the image of God because we are like God and we represent Him.

Have you ever seen a movie that was set in ancient Rome? If so, you've probably watched Roman soldiers march off to war. At least one of the men will be carrying an eagle on a pole. The eagle represents Rome, just as the army represents the military power of Rome. You might also see a man carrying a flag on a pole. The flag and the image embroidered on it are an *ensign*, an emblem representing the emperor.

We are the ensigns of God—images representing Him. When God said to Adam and Eve, "Be fruitful and multiply. Fill the earth and govern it. Reign over the fish in the sea, the birds in the sky, and all the animals that scurry along the ground" (Genesis 1:28), He gave humankind dominion over the earth. We are to rule in His stead, as His representatives.

Some say being created in God's image means that we have an innate sense of right and wrong. Others say it means that we are aware of time. Still others, that we have emotions. Or that we have souls.

Regardless, we carry His authority as we go into the world. We are to rule and act as God's image bearers. We are to bring Him glory as we live and love and teach and raise our families and make our livings.

What an honor! What a responsibility! And how tragic for those who do not realize why they have been created.

Wayne Grudem reminds us of the importance of this realization:

> We must remember that even fallen, sinful man has the *status*
> of being in God's image. . . . Every single human being, no
> matter how much the image of God is marred by sin, or ill-
> ness, or weakness, or age, or any other disability, still has the
> *status* of being in God's image and therefore must be treated
> with the dignity and respect that is due to God's image-bearer.
> This has profound implications for our conduct toward others.
> It means that people of every race deserve equal dignity and
> rights. It means that elderly people, those seriously ill, the
> mentally retarded, and children yet unborn, deserve full pro-
> tection and honor as human beings. If we ever deny our
> unique status in creation as God's only image-bearers, we will
> soon begin to depreciate the value of human life, will tend to
> see humans as merely a higher form of animal, and will begin
> to treat others as such. We will also lose much of our sense of
> meaning in life.[16]

In the culture around us, we see a concerted effort to deny that humans are representatives of God. Teachers and philosophers and politicians would have you believe that humans are simply the top of the animal kingdom, the apex of an evolutionary process. They teach that people are animals and often proclaim that animal rights should equal human rights, while ignoring the fact that animals are not created in the image of God but men and women are! We are to be benevolent rulers of the animal kingdom, never abusing or mis-using them, yes. But one thing is clear: God never intended for humans and animals to have equal dominance over the earth.

When men and women are considered mere animals, it becomes easier to kill the wounded, abort unborn babies, and eliminate the handicapped or aged. Life is no longer a gift from God but rather a happy twist of fate.

You are not an animal; you are a man or woman, created to be God's image bearer on earth. You are to demonstrate your Creator's communicable attributes (the qualities we can emulate to some extent), such as truth, virtue, love, wisdom, holiness, and righteousness.

Do you have the gift of speaking? Then speak as though God himself were speaking through you. Do you have the gift of helping others? Do it with all the strength and energy that God supplies. Then everything you do will bring glory to God through Jesus Christ. All glory and power to him forever and ever! Amen. (1 Peter 4:11)

You are to live your life using the personality and talents God gave you, because who doesn't enjoy doing the things he or she was created to do? If God gave you an exceptional voice, He wants you to sing! If He gave you a gift for stringing words together, string them into a book! Likewise, if He gave you an ability to make money, make it and invest it wisely. (The Bible has a lot to say about using money wisely; apparently He has been generous with this gift.) If He gave you the gift of empathy, encourage and comfort others. If He gave you multiple gifts, invest them in the opportunities He sends your way. You may not always sing or write or invest or teach or run or dance, but God will lead you through the right doors in His perfect timing. As we are exhorted in 1 Corinthians 10:31, "Whether you eat or drink, or whatever you do, do it all for the glory of God."

TO THINK ABOUT

1. Have you ever considered what it means to be created in the image of God? What did it mean to you before reading this? Did your view change? How should this reality affect the way we live in the world?

2. The beliefs of our increasingly secular world are often subtle, but they are completely opposite of what the Bible tells us about people and our Creator. What situations have you seen lately that exalt humankind over God? That equate humans with animals or humans with the earth? We may not see people worshipping statues of birds and animals, but we certainly see people worshipping nature. We are to be good stewards of the earth but not worshippers of it.

> God shows his anger from heaven against all sinful, wicked
> people who suppress the truth by their wickedness. They know
> the truth about God because he has made it obvious to them.
> For ever since the world was created, people have seen the
> earth and sky. Through everything God made, they can clearly
> see his invisible qualities—his eternal power and divine nature.
> So they have no excuse for not knowing God.
>   Yes, they knew God, but they wouldn't worship him as
> God or even give him thanks. And they began to think up
> foolish ideas of what God was like. As a result, their minds be-
> came dark and confused. Claiming to be wise, they instead be-
> came utter fools. And instead of worshiping the glorious,
> ever-living God, they worshiped idols made to look like mere
> people and birds and animals and reptiles. (Romans 1:18–23)

Look around you—what have you seen that qualifies as idol worship?

3. What is your purpose on earth? Have you always had a clear view of it? What gifts has God given you? Have you developed those gifts?

Gifts rarely appear fully developed. God gives us certain abilities and entrusts us with the responsibility of developing them. Whatever your talents are, He wants you to use them to bring Him glory because your gifts originated with Him.

How can you develop your gifts this week?

4. Have you ever wondered why God created the universe? God the Father, the Son, and the Holy Spirit existed along with millions of created angels, and at some point in time, God said, "Let us make human beings" (Genesis 1:26).

Does thinking about the eternality and power of God make you feel small? It should. But when you think about how amazing it is that this great God made a way for you and me to live with Him in holy fellowship forever . . . the mind boggles.

He created us with the freedom to choose, knowing we would choose to sin. So, as far back as the Garden of Eden, He announced the plan for redemption (3:15), and the Son agreed. Audacious love. Amazing, undeserved grace.

How does a proper understanding of humanity's role in God's universe change your perspective? How can you share this understanding with your family and friends?

5. The world around us is challenged by racism, political squabbles, and issues of life and death, such as abortion and euthanasia. Having a proper view of why humans were created would end these struggles—all men and women, no matter what race, *could become* God's ambassadors. All humans, born and unborn, could choose to be God's representatives. All children, healthy and otherwise, are made in the image of God. Every life has a purpose.

What are some things you can do this week to fulfill your purpose as God's image bearer? How can you share this purpose with those around you?

Most important, how can you encourage someone who might be depressed, someone who has never realized who she is in God's sight?

When I look at the night sky and see the work of your
    fingers—
the moon and the stars you set in place—
what are mere mortals that you should think about them,
    human beings that you should care for them?
Yet you made them only a little lower than God
    and crowned them with glory and honor.
You gave them charge of everything you made,
    putting all things under their authority. (Psalm 8:3–6)

Six

THE BRIDEGROOM

SEEING RICK RIVERS, MY soon-to-be husband, dressed in a tuxedo and standing tall and handsome at the front of the church, waiting for me, I counted myself the most fortunate woman on the planet. Fifty years later, we look at our wedding pictures and chuckle at how starry-eyed we both were. We're still starry-eyed in some ways, though we've been through stormy times.

Recently I asked Rick what his greatest concerns had been before our wedding. He said that most of them had to do with whether he could protect and provide for his wife in a manner he thought worthy of her. He had no questions or fears about the vows: to love and cherish in sickness and in health, for richer and poorer until death parts us. And I certainly have no complaints about the manner in which he has supported me. I can't count the number of times he's said, "Nothing ventured, nothing gained," when I've been hesitant or downright chicken about trying something new, including starting a writing career. (I never would have sent in the first manuscript if he hadn't said those words.)

The word *bridegroom* brings many things to mind, some not popular in our current culture. I wanted Rick to be the head of our household. That did not mean I wouldn't have a voice in our relationship. It didn't mean I was enslaved or subordinate. I knew my place was beside him, an equal with a different role.

In God's plan, the bridegroom initiates his bride into the physical aspect of married life. In the law of the Old Testament, the bridegroom was to stay home for a full year to "give happiness to his wife" (Deuteronomy 24:5, NASB). He wasn't to be sent off to war. Part of that happiness undoubtedly had to do with fathering a child. A husband was to be a living example to his wife and children of godly living. Just as Christ is the head of the church, a man is to be the head of his family (Ephesians 5:23). That's not an easy responsibility when you consider that Christ died for us. A man takes on that willingness to sacrifice himself for the good of his wife and children. I'm fortunate to be married to a man who knows that ideal and strives to uphold it.

Unfortunately, in our modern world, bridegrooms don't get a year to give their wives happiness before being called away. Rick and I had a few weeks of bliss, and then the Marine Corps gave him new orders. We had barely moved into our one-room flat off base when he was deployed to Yuma, Arizona. Though I was thankful the orders weren't sending him off on a second tour in Vietnam, three weeks apart seemed like an eternity to a new bride and groom. I think of the women waiting for their husbands who are serving overseas for a year or more. Separation is never easy. I remember the longing I felt for my husband to be with me. We remained in contact through telephone calls, but they weren't as wonderful as having Rick by my side.

Jesus is called the Bridegroom in Scripture. He was born of a woman who had humanity's sin nature, but in His thirty-three years of living among humankind, He never had an evil thought or committed an evil deed. He was as holy then as He had been in the Garden of Eden at Creation and as He will be in eternity.

Jesus lived a life of perfection, then paid the bride-price—death—for us so we can belong to Him through faith. He was buried for three days and defeated death through His own power. At the moment of His death, the bridal veil that separated the holy of holies from the people was torn from top to bottom, revealing the way for people to have a renewed, personal, intimate relationship with almighty God.

Jesus ascended into heaven after promising to send His Holy Spirit to those who belong to Him. When we are baptized, we publicly say "I do!" to Jesus. He sends His Holy Spirit to dwell in us when we accept Him. That Spirit remains within us, a sacred seal of identity, like a wedding ring that promises eternity with our Bridegroom. The Holy Spirit opens our minds and hearts as He whispers enlightenment and encouragement to us. The Spirit leads us to instructions in His Word and guides us through the trials of our earthly lives. In the physical sense, Jesus, our husband, is away, deployed to be our advocate before almighty God. In the spiritual sense, He is always with us, wedded to us. He will be with us to the end of time.

It's difficult for us to believe in what we cannot see. God is close to us. He speaks to us through His Word, the Bible, and through His creation. He doesn't shout, like so many in our world do. He doesn't argue or debate. He whispers His love and truth. And His Son, vigilant as our constant intercessor, waits for God's signal that it's time to fetch His bride.

As believers, we long for the return of our Bridegroom. We ache for Him to make things right in this fallen world. We feel the anticipation, and we hope for His quick return. Then we will welcome Him—like the soldier-husband who's been away too long—with love and passion, thanksgiving and gratitude. The physical separation will be over.

Believers (the bride) will experience the eternal life He promised, for our Groom will come in power, destroying all evil, bringing purity and purpose, a new heaven and new earth, and a life filled with health and beauty and joy. By His strength and through His love, we will be carried over the threshold of this fallen world into the flawless new world He created, which was intended to be our home from the beginning.

Instinctively, all of us long to return to the Garden of Eden as it was before the Fall. From the beginning, every soul was meant for eternity. Our souls are still eternal. Each of us must make a personal choice about where we want to spend our eternal lives: in heaven or hell. The questions are simple: In whom will you put your faith? With whom do you want to spend eternity? With God, who created you to fellowship with Him in love? Or with Satan, who lies in order to deceive you and separate you from God?

The choice is yours.

Faithful and True

I am overwhelmed with joy in the LORD my God!
For he has dressed me with the clothing of salvation
and draped me in a robe of righteousness.
I am like a bridegroom dressed for his wedding
or a bride with her jewels.

ISAIAH 61:10

"MIRIAM SENT ME *to find you, Amanda. I want to take you home."*
He meant it.

Amanda. Her throat closed, and she smiled. Another burden lifted,
and she was grateful, but it wasn't that easy or simple. She couldn't let
it be. "I can't go back, Paul. Not ever."

"Why not?"

How much did he have to know to understand and become her
ally? "There's a lot about me you still don't know."

"Then tell me."

She chewed on her lip. How much was enough? "I was sold into
prostitution when I was eight," she said slowly, staring down at noth-
ing. "I never knew any other way of life until Michael married me."
She looked at him again. "And I never understood him, not the way
he hoped I would. I can't change who I was. I can't undo the things
that happened."

Paul leaned forward. "You're the one who still doesn't understand,
Amanda. There's something I didn't even comprehend until now be-

cause I was too stubborn and jealous and proud . . . Michael chose
you. With all your past, with all your frailties, with everything. He
knew from the beginning where you came from, and it didn't make
any difference to him. There were plenty of women back home who
would have jumped at the chance to marry him. Sweet, sensible virgin
girls from God-fearing families. He never fell in love with any of them.
He took one look at you, and he knew. *Right from the beginning. You.*
No one else. He told me all that, but I thought it was sex. Now I know
it wasn't. It was something else."

"A crazy accident—"

"I think it's because he knew how much you needed him."

⚜

In the House of Magdalena, Angel gave Paul the hard truth—a
truth she had never shared with him before. In return, Paul gifted
Angel a corresponding truth—something he had never understood
before but exactly what Angel needed to hear. She needed to know
that Michael had chosen her. And God had chosen her for Michael.

This excerpt could be talking about Jesus and me . . . and you.
He chose us. Before the beginning of the world, our faithful and
true Bridegroom chose us to be His bride. "You didn't choose me,"
Jesus said. "I chose you. I appointed you to go and produce lasting
fruit, so that the Father will give you whatever you ask for, using my
name" (John 15:16).

Even before he made the world, God loved us and chose us in
Christ to be holy and without fault in his eyes. God decided in
advance to adopt us into his own family by bringing us to
himself through Jesus Christ. This is what he wanted to do,
and it gave him great pleasure. So we praise God for the glorious grace he has poured out on us who belong to his dear Son.
He is so rich in kindness and grace that he purchased our free-

dom with the blood of his Son and forgave our sins. (Ephesians 1:4–7)

Our faithful Bridegroom betrothed Himself to us even before the world was created. He knew us; He knew where we would come from; He knew our frailties and our sins. And those things didn't make any difference to Him. He knew how much we would need Him, so He chose us and died for us, buying our freedom by paying the price for our sin with His own precious blood.

The Hebrew word *chathan* (pronounced khaw-THAWN), meaning "bridegroom," and the corresponding Greek word *numphios* (pronounced noom-FEE-awss) are found in both the Old and New Testaments. As we have already seen in the Old Testament, God frequently referred to Israel as His chosen bride. In most modern weddings, the bride gets all the attention, and every eye is focused on her as she comes down the aisle. In the biblical wedding, however, Jesus is the bridegroom, and the attention is rightfully focused on Him. He deserves all the honor and praise and glory. He did all the work, and if the bride has any beauty, it's because He has cleansed and preserved her.

> For husbands, this means love your wives, just as Christ loved
> the church. He gave up his life for her to make her holy and
> clean, washed by the cleansing of God's word. He did this to
> present her to himself as a glorious church without a spot or
> wrinkle or any other blemish. Instead, she will be holy and
> without fault. (5:25–27)

Though Hosea often must have wondered about Gomer's loyalty, he was determined to be a faithful husband. He did not stray, did not visit the sacred prostitutes, and did not take his marital problems to another understanding woman. He had married Gomer and promised to be faithful and true.

Since Jesus is part of the Godhead, He shares the attributes of

God. Among those attributes is faithfulness. His character and purpose do not change. He never becomes better or worse. He has emotions and expresses them, but He always loves what He loves and always hates what He hates. He loves you. He hates sin. Those two emotions will never change.

> May the God of peace make you holy in every way, and may your whole spirit and soul and body be kept blameless until our Lord Jesus Christ comes again. God will make this happen, for he who calls you is faithful. (1 Thessalonians 5:23–24)

> The faithful love of the LORD never ends!
>> His mercies never cease.
> Great is his faithfulness;
>> his mercies begin afresh each morning. (Lamentations 3:22–23)

Jesus, the Bridegroom, is also *true*. He does not lie; He does not deceive. Jesus keeps His word. The Bridegroom can always be trusted.

> God is not a man, so he does not lie.
>> He is not human, so he does not change his mind.
> Has he ever spoken and failed to act?
>> Has he ever promised and not carried it through?
>> (Numbers 23:19)

Truth is a fundamental element of God's personality. Jesus is the Word of God who is "full of grace and truth" (John 1:14, NKJV). The Holy Spirit is called "the Spirit of truth" (14:17, NKJV).

> Jesus told him, "I am the way, the truth, and the life. No one can come to the Father except through me." (verse 6)

For the truth about anything, turn to the Word of God. The truths the Holy Spirit imparted through those who wrote the Scriptures are the bottom line for any question you may have about God, people, redemption, society, history, sin, and the meaning of life. Do not listen to those who would declare the Bible an ancient book riddled with errors. It has been miraculously preserved through the ages, and Jesus Himself quoted from the Old Testament Scriptures to prove their trustworthiness.

> Above all, you must realize that no prophecy in Scripture ever came from the prophet's own understanding, or from human initiative. No, those prophets were moved by the Holy Spirit, and they spoke from God. (2 Peter 1:20–21)

The Bible tells us that Hosea had to speak hard truths to the people of Israel. Without soft-pedaling or worrying about being politically correct, he told them that their sin would result in exile and punishment but that when they returned to God and confessed their sin, He would forgive them and bring them back to their land. They would be restored.

Finding anyone who consistently tells the truth is a challenge today. People lie all the time—on their tax returns, to their friends and neighbors, to their bosses, to their spouses. A friend of mine recently had some work done on her house, and she was shocked at how many construction workers told her to lie about the amount of work being done so they wouldn't have to pull a permit. We have learned to be skeptical of everything we hear, even from media and our government.

But God does not lie, and He does not want us to lie either. You could make a case for lying in a situation like the one faced by the Hebrew midwives—they lied to Pharaoh so they wouldn't have to murder innocent babies (Exodus 1:15–19). But most of us are not facing life-or-death situations when we tell lies.

I am convinced of one thing: telling the truth honors God. A bridegroom who tells his bride the truth honors her as well.

TO THINK ABOUT

1. What does it mean for a bridegroom to be faithful and true? The word *faithful* means more than "not committing adultery." It refers to having consistent character, where the bridegroom's commitment to love does not change.

How did Michael Hosea demonstrate God's character in *Redeeming Love*? He was not bland or passionless; he was often upset and agonized by Angel's decisions. But did her actions make him stop loving her? Did he ever give up on her?

Why do you think it took Angel so long to recognize this aspect of Michael's character? Why is faithfulness a rare quality in our society?

2. Did Michael ever lie to Angel? How often do you lie? Do you bend the truth without thinking? Can you force yourself to become more aware of the little lies that slip past your lips? God is truth, and He does not lie. He will honor you if you make this effort to always tell the truth. (If telling the truth might harm someone, be silent.)

I [Jesus] tell you this, you must give an account on judgment day for every idle word you speak. (Matthew 12:36)

In your notebook, write down any lies that have slipped past your lips today, no matter how trivial or harmless. Make an effort to correct those with truth if you can. And tomorrow be mindful of the words that come out of your mouth—may they all be truthful.

3. Have you known men and women who could be described as faithful and true, who exhibit those qualities every day? Most people aren't born with those noble qualities, so where do they come from?

When we accept Christ and determine to follow Him, the Holy

Spirit resides in us—we become a temple for the third person of the Godhead. He teaches us, leads us, and prays for us as we live in His power.

Remember the parable of the farmer sowing his seed (Mark 4:3–20)? When we follow Christ, we are that fourth kind of seed, the seed that lands on good soil and puts down roots. We grow and flourish, and the Holy Spirit quickens us so we bear fruit: "love, joy, peace, patience, kindness, goodness, faithfulness, gentleness, and self-control" (Galatians 5:22–23). That's how we have access to God's faithfulness. That's how we become like Michael and Hosea and Jesus.

How can you display the fruit of the Spirit today?

4. When you are depressed, discouraged, or exhausted, find a quiet place to sit and reflect on the faithfulness of God. You may be in a momentary lull, but God is not. If you belong to Him, He will never leave you, never forsake you, and never break a promise in His Word. He will strengthen you, uphold you, forgive you, encourage you, and guide you in the right path.

Ask Him to calm your spirit, refresh your soul, and keep your mind focused on His goodness and faithfulness. He will never fail you.

In your notebook, describe several ways God has demonstrated His faithfulness to you.

5. We humans are often at the mercy of our emotions. Depression hits and the entire world seems bleak. Happiness bubbles up and everything is wonderful. Anger boils over and something short-circuits in our brains. We do and say things we thought we would never say or do.

God is not like us in that regard. His emotions are consistent. His love for us is unchanging, and so is His hate for sin.

What would God be like if His emotions were as fickle as ours?

Could we trust a God like that? Could we be certain of our status with Him if He were as changeable as we are?

Take a moment to write down a prayer of thanksgiving that God is God . . . and not like us.

Great is Thy faithfulness, O God my Father—
There is no shadow of turning with Thee!
Thou changest not—Thy compassions, they fail not.
As Thou hast been Thou forever wilt be.

Great is Thy faithfulness!
Great is Thy faithfulness!
Morning by morning new mercies I see.
All I have needed Thy hand hath provided—
Great is Thy faithfulness, Lord, unto me.[17]

STUDY 6.2

Loving and Holy

*My generation was taught to sing, "What the world needs
now is love, sweet love," in which we robustly instruct the
Almighty that we do not need another mountain (we
have enough of them), but we could do with some more
love. The hubris is staggering.*

D. A. CARSON, *THE DIFFICULT DOCTRINE*

OF THE LOVE OF GOD

MICHAEL KNEW ALL *the possible motives for Amanda's desertion.
But beyond that, beyond comprehension, he knew God's will was
working. "Why this way?" he cried out in anguish. "Why did you tell
me to love her if you were only going to take her away from me?"*

*He raged at God and grieved for his wife. He stopped reading his
Bible. He stopped praying. He turned inside himself seeking answers.
He found none. And he dreamed, dark, confusing dreams with forces
that were closing in on him.*

*The still, quiet voice didn't speak to him anymore, not for weeks
and months. God was silent and hidden, his purpose a mystery. Life
became such a barren wasteland that Michael couldn't bear it anymore, and he cried out.*

"Why have you forsaken me?"

Beloved, I am always with you, even to the end of time.

Michael slowed his frenetic work and sought solace in God's word.
I don't understand anything anymore, Lord. Losing her is like los-

ing half of myself. She loved me. I know she did. Why did you drive her from me?

The answer came to him slowly, with the changing of the seasons.

You shall have no other gods before me.

That couldn't be right.

Michael's anger grew. "When have I worshiped anyone but you?" *He raged again.* "I've followed you all my life. I've never *put anyone before you.*" *Hands fisted, he wept.* "I love her, but I never made her my god."

In the calm that followed his angry torrent of words, Michael heard—and finally understood.

You became hers.

⚜

G od's love—such simple words yet so profoundly misunderstood. The world sings that we need more love, that all we need is love, and that love makes the world go 'round.[18]

God poured out a river of love for us to immerse ourselves in, but few people do.

Why? Because we can't pick and choose the aspects of God we want to enjoy. We can't say, "I'll take two helpings of love, one helping of mercy, but hold the holiness, the wrath, and the judgment."

God is a complex being with many attributes: He is omnipotent (all-powerful), omnipresent (everywhere present), omniscient (all-knowing), eternal, and infinite (with no beginning and no end). He is self-existent and self-supporting. He is consistent. He is holy and righteous, just and true. He is filled with grace and mercy. He is sovereign—in control of all creation, every dimension and time. He is perfection.

Because Jesus is God, He shares all God's attributes, all those qualities. The Prince of Peace is also the one who will judge the world for sin.

The Father judges no one. Instead, he has given the Son absolute authority to judge, so that everyone will honor the Son, just as they honor the Father. Anyone who does not honor the Son is certainly not honoring the Father who sent him.

I tell you the truth, those who listen to my message and believe in God who sent me have eternal life. They will never be condemned for their sins, but they have already passed from death into life.

And I assure you that the time is coming, indeed it's here now, when the dead will hear my voice—the voice of the Son of God. And those who listen will live. The Father has life in himself, and he has granted that same life-giving power to his Son. And he has given him authority to judge everyone because he is the Son of Man. Don't be so surprised! Indeed, the time is coming when all the dead in their graves will hear the voice of God's Son, and they will rise again. Those who have done good will rise to experience eternal life, and those who have continued in evil will rise to experience judgment. (John 5:22–29)

Everyone wants to think of a bridegroom as loving, but God's love, while perfect and eternal and unchanging, coexists with His holiness. God cannot tolerate sin. God is love, and He always loves what He loves. He hates sin, and He always hates what He hates.

I know this statement is cliché today, but it's true: God loves the sinner and hates the sin. He invites sinners to come to Him, confess their sins, cast them off, and enter into a full and loving relationship with Him.

But too many people want God's love *without* abandoning their sin.

I love my grandchildren no matter where they are or what they are doing. But if they have been playing outside in the mud, I do not want them to come into the house until they take off their shoes on the front-porch mat. Once they've taken off their dirty shoes, they can come into the house so we can spend a wonderful day together.

I love them whether they are inside or outside the house, but if they want to curl up in my lap and read books or bake cookies or do any of the things that grandkids do with their grandmas, they're going to have to come inside with clean feet.

Likewise, if you want to be welcomed into God's presence, you'll need to leave the mud—the sin—behind.

Will everything be perfect after that? Once you've kicked off those muddy shoes, will life be free and easy? You might think so, but God sees things from a different perspective.

Consider the novel excerpt—Michael was grieving, miserable, and frustrated. He didn't understand why God had allowed Angel to leave him. Michael wasn't sinning, not even when he was so frustrated he couldn't pray or read his Bible. God understands our emotions. That's one of the reasons Jesus came to live as a man—so He would understand our emotions from the perspective of our human weakness (Hebrews 4:15).

From God's perspective, Michael had been obedient; he had done everything God asked him to do. Hosea did everything God wanted him to do for Gomer, and she still left him.

We don't often see things from God's perspective. We get so caught up in our concerns and emotions that we fail to wonder *why* God might be allowing us to go through difficult situations.

But you can rest in this: *God is sovereign.* There is no situation, no time, when the world slips out of His control. He doesn't take naps. Satan can't put God out of commission. Nothing that happens to you can surprise Him. The promotion you were denied, the death in the family, the broken heart, the cancer diagnosis, the accident, the betrayal by your friend—God knew about all those things before they happened. And although you may be so caught up in your concerns and emotions that you are not even *thinking* about God's plan, you can trust that He has one. He still loves you, and He will keep His promises and hold you in the palm of His hand.

When bad things happen, model your attitude after Hosea and Michael, who suffered but did not stop believing in God.

Remember Job? A God-fearing man from the land of Uz, Job had seven sons and three daughters. He had great wealth, good health, and a wife. But one day Satan asked God for permission to test Job, and God said, "Go ahead" (Job 1:12).

So bandits stole Job's oxen and donkeys. The same day, fire fell from heaven and burned up his sheep, and bands of Chaldean raiders took his camels and killed his servants. Then, worst of all, Job's sons and daughters were banqueting at the oldest brother's home when a mighty wind struck the house. The building collapsed and all Job's children died (verses 13–19).

Job's wealth—gone.

Job's beloved children—gone.

At least he still had his health and his wife.

But a little later, Satan received permission to afflict Job with painful boils from the sole of his foot to the top of his head (2:6–7). Have you ever been tormented by an insect bite? Multiply that pain by a thousand, and you can only begin to imagine what Job endured. Instead of comforting him, Job's wife looked at him and said, "Are you still holding firmly to your integrity? Curse God and die!" (verse 9, TLV).

I think I understand why Satan didn't take Job's wife.

Job faced destruction in every area of his life, but the Bible tells us that "through all this, Job did not sin nor did he cast reproach on God" (1:22, TLV).

In the end, Job was rewarded for his steadfast confidence in God. The Lord doubled everything he had lost. At the end of his days, he had fourteen thousand sheep, six thousand camels, one thousand yoke of oxen, and one thousand female donkeys. He also had seven sons and three daughters (42:10–13), along with the seven sons and three daughters in heaven. "Nowhere in the land," the Bible tells us, "were there found women as beautiful as the daughters of Job" (verse 15, TLV).

Our Bridegroom loves you always, even when you are so sorrowful you can't feel anything. He loves you when frustration grips you and when you question His reasons. He loves you when confusion swirls around you.

He loves you so much that when you are facing your bleakest hour, He is in heaven praying for you: "Who then will condemn us? No one—for Christ Jesus died for us and was raised to life for us, and he is sitting in the place of honor at God's right hand, pleading for us" (Romans 8:34).

TO THINK ABOUT

1. The Christian life is not guaranteed to be easy. Some describe it as a spiritual boot camp where we endure trials and tribulations in order to strengthen our faith. James, a half brother of Jesus, wrote, "Dear brothers and sisters, when troubles of any kind come your way, consider it an opportunity for great joy. For you know that when your faith is tested, your endurance has a chance to grow. So let it grow, for when your endurance is fully developed, you will be perfect and complete, needing nothing" (James 1:2–4).

Do not think your life will go smoothly once you surrender it to Jesus, but know this: the Lord will always be with you, upholding you and giving you the strength you need to get through whatever test or trial you are called to endure. The Holy Spirit will guide and teach you, and the Lord will bring people across your path—people to encourage you and some you may need to encourage. Who has encouraged you in your faith walk? Whom might you need to encourage? How can you do that?

2. Our Bridegroom is holy. If you fall into sin, the Holy Spirit will convict you. If you confess your sin, Jesus will forgive you. When He died, He died for your future sins because you did not yet exist. *All* your sins have been forgiven, so once you belong to Christ, you need not worry about a sin sending you to hell. "There is no condemnation for those who belong to Christ Jesus. And because you belong to him, the power of the life-giving Spirit has freed you from the power of sin that leads to death" (Romans 8:1–2).

Sin blocks the fellowship between you and God because when you sin, you are obeying your own selfish desires instead of obeying God. "If I had not confessed the sin in my heart, the Lord would not have listened" (Psalm 66:18). Sin is never inconsequential; it always damages. So do not forget that our loving Bridegroom is holy and forgiveness is never free. It always costs the one who forgives.

If my friend breaks a precious vase that once belonged to my mother, I will forgive her, but I have lost something that meant a great deal to me. If someone spreads vicious rumors about you and later begs for forgiveness, you can and should forgive her, but your reputation has been damaged.

What is the true cost of forgiveness? How did Jesus bear this cost? How do you bear it when you forgive? Who forgave *you* for something, and what did that forgiveness cost?

3. Throughout history, many Christians have experienced what has come to be known as the "dark night of the soul." Michael experienced it. The prophet Jeremiah also experienced it. Job experienced it. Jesus experienced it, I believe, in Gethsemane.

It's a time when everything seems to work against you and when God seems far, far away. But though you cannot see Him or hear Him and your prayers seem to go no higher than the ceiling, do not lose faith. Do not lose courage. Do not give up. Because on the other side of this dark night lies a new morning.

Read Psalm 88, which seems to have been written when the psalmist was having a dark night of the soul. It is a psalm of desperation. Some theologians believe it is messianic because it speaks of situations that are much like what Jesus endured in Gethsemane and during His crucifixion.

After you read Psalm 88, read Psalm 89. This is the song for the morning after.

Have you ever had a dark night of the soul? What was the situation? How did God resolve the problem? What did you learn from the experience, and how are you different today because of it?

4. Some people have trouble accepting the doctrine of God's sovereignty because they say it makes human beings mere puppets in the hands of God. They claim it makes a mockery of people's free will.

I once heard a thought that cleared up the confusion for me: God's sovereignty can be illustrated by the metaphor of a writer and his story. The writer writes the story and directs the characters, but inside the story world, the characters live and move and have free will *on their level.* They are not the author, and most of them don't even know the author exists.

In our world, we live and move and have free will on our human level. But our free will does not give us unlimited power. We can't do whatever we want to do, because we are limited by laws of nature. I can't step outside and fly no matter how much I want to. My level of freedom is limited by what I am.

God's freedom is unlimited because He is God. He can do anything with His creation—and His story—that He wills. That doesn't make me a mindless puppet; it makes me a *mindful character* who knows her place in creation.

Think about the sovereignty of God. Everything we are, everything we have done, and everything we will do is part of God's plan for us. He controls the universe, the planet, the government, the king or president, our neighbors, our employers, our health. So when something unfavorable happens to us, we may be upset, but we can rest in this: God is in charge.

In your notebook, write down several unfavorable things that have happened to you recently. Now, next to each of them, write *God is in control.*

This realization is so liberating!

5. Are you bearing a grudge against anyone today? Maybe someone who wronged you? If he or she is aware of your anger, write a letter to let the person know that you have forgiven the wrongdoing. If the perpetrator is not aware, go before the Lord and lay that offense at His feet. In your notebook, write a message of forgiveness for that person, and if you are ever tempted to pick up that grudge again, pull out your notebook and reread that message.

Forgiveness is freedom!

She who cannot forgive destroys the bridge over which she herself must pass, for everyone needs to be forgiven.[19]

STUDY 6.3

Willing to Redeem

*The Father loves me because I sacrifice my life so I may
take it back again. No one can take my life from me. I
sacrifice it voluntarily. For I have the authority to lay it
down when I want to and also to take it up again. For
this is what my Father has commanded.*

JOHN 10:17–18

MICHAEL COULDN'T GET *Angel out of his mind. He tried to con-
centrate on his work and found himself thinking about her instead.
Why did she keep eating at him? Why did he have this gut feeling that
something was wrong? He worked until past dark every day and then
sat before the fire, tormented with thoughts of her. He saw her face in
the flames, beckoning to him. To hell itself, no doubt. Or was he getting a taste of that already?*

*He remembered the tragic air about her as she had passed him that
first day, and then reminded himself how hard-hearted she was. He
swore he wouldn't go back to her, then did so every night when he slept
and Angel haunted his dreams. He couldn't escape her. She danced
before him, like Salome before King Herod. He would reach out for
her, and she would move back, tantalizing him.* You want me, don't
you, Michael? Then come back. Come back.

*After a few days, his dreams turned to nightmares. She was fleeing
from something. He ran after her, calling out for her to stop, but she*

*ran on until she came to a ledge. She looked back at him then, the
wind whipping her golden hair about her white face.*

Mara, wait!

She turned away and spread her arms wide and went over.

"No!" *Michael awakened with a start, his body streaming sweat.
His chest heaved; his heart raced so fast his body shook with it. He
raked trembling hands through his hair. "Jesus," he whispered into the
darkness. "Jesus, deliver me from this." Why did she haunt him so?*

*He got up and opened the door, leaning heavily against the frame.
It was raining again. He closed his eyes wearily. He hadn't prayed in
days. "I'd be a fool to go back," he said aloud. "A fool." He looked out
at the dark, weeping sky again. "But that's what you want, isn't it,
Lord? And you're not going to give me any peace until I do."*

*He sighed heavily and rubbed the back of his neck. "I don't see
what good will come of it, but I'll go back, Lord. I don't like it much,
but I'll do what you want." When he finally went back to bed, he slept
deeply and without dreaming for the first time in days.*

*In the morning, the sky was clear. Michael loaded the wagon and
hitched up the team.*

⁂

Michael had to struggle with reality and second thoughts before getting into his wagon and driving into Pair-a-Dice to
redeem Angel. The last time he'd seen her, she'd made it clear she
wanted nothing to do with him. She didn't want to be married. She
was the last person on earth he would have chosen for a wife.

But God had chosen her for him. And Michael recognized God's
insistent voice, so he obeyed.

When Adam and Eve sinned in the Garden of Eden, God told
them He would send a redeemer to conquer the Evil One (Genesis
3:15). Jesus was that redeemer. He understood His mission before

His human birth and as a child. The Bible tells us that by the time He was twelve, He was meeting with rabbis in the temple and confounding them with His knowledge (Luke 2:42–47).

But even though He knew His mission, His human nature resisted the thought of the pain ahead. He struggled with knowing that thousands of people, born and as yet unborn, would want nothing to do with Him. They wouldn't want to surrender. They wouldn't want His forgiveness. Some of them would repeatedly spurn His love, resisting Him until it was too late.

And then there was the physical pain. Crucifixion was probably the most excruciating way a person could die. The death, which He would experience in a human body, would be neither quick nor merciful. Hanging by the roadside as a public example, beaten, naked, mocked, and with nails supporting His weight at His feet and wrists—who could accept that destiny without a struggle?

Jesus was not immune to emotions:

> Accompanied by the disciples, Jesus left the upstairs room and
> went as usual to the Mount of Olives. There he told them,
> "Pray that you will not give in to temptation."
> He walked away, about a stone's throw, and knelt down
> and prayed, "Father, if you are willing, please take this cup of
> suffering away from me. Yet I want your will to be done, not
> mine." Then an angel from heaven appeared and strengthened
> him. He prayed more fervently, and he was in such agony of
> spirit that his sweat fell to the ground like great drops of
> blood.
> At last he stood up again and returned to the disciples, only
> to find them asleep, exhausted from grief. (Luke 22:39–45)

I don't know whether any human can fully imagine what it must have been like for Jesus, the second member of the Godhead, to set aside His glory and come down to be born as a frail, helpless baby. He was fully God and fully man, which meant He experienced all the things we humans experience: skinned knees and childhood illnesses, sorrow and joy, delight and disappointment.

The Jews were expecting their messiah, but they were not expecting the epitome of self-sacrifice. Not a simple man who grew up in the poor home of a carpenter. This man, this Jesus, began His ministry at the age of thirty, walking among the poor and lowly in Galilee, touching untouchables, eating with tax collectors, forgiving sinners. And when He reached the end of His three-year ministry, He knew the time had come for Him to sacrifice Himself for all humankind.

As God, Jesus knew everything that would happen to Him. He knew His disciples would scatter. He knew Peter would betray Him. He knew His mother's heart would be broken. He knew His followers would doubt everything He had ever told them. He knew they would grieve.

He knew the chief priests and elders would rejoice to see Him gone. He knew the skies would darken and the earth would quake. He knew His death would coincide with the slaughter of the Passover lambs at the temple, but few people in Jerusalem would realize the Lamb of God was being slain for the sins of the world.

But He also knew the Roman centurion would see Him and believe He was the Son of God. He knew the second thief would also believe and join Him in paradise, the waiting place beyond the grave. He knew the veil in the temple would be torn, opening the way for all people, not only the priests, to obtain access to God the Father.

Unless Jesus died, all the sons and daughters of Adam and Eve would spend eternity apart from God, in a place where there is no light, no color, no beauty, no goodness, no love, no joy, no freedom—nothing that flows from God.

So although Jesus's human body dreaded the coming pain, He welcomed the sacrifice, the humiliation, and the agony. God's plan, His will, would be worth it all.

Michael did *not* have the mind of God and could not see the future, but he had faith. He trusted in God, so he obeyed that inner voice that sent him after Angel. Because he had faith, Angel's life was changed and she became a new creation in Christ.

TO THINK ABOUT

1. Angel is a fictional character, but she represents millions of real people who have given their broken lives to Jesus and found new lives on the other side of surrender.

Why do you think this story has the power to change lives even when it's about fictional characters? Has a novel ever changed your life? If so, which novel, and how did it influence you?

2. Some of the universal truths of *Redeeming Love* come straight from the Bible:

- "The wages of sin is death, but the free gift of God is eternal life through Christ Jesus our Lord" (Romans 6:23). We have *all* sinned, and we have all earned death because none of us is holy. None of us deserves a future in heaven or an abundant life as God's child.

- "God showed his great love for us by sending Christ to die for us while we were still sinners" (5:8). Angel came to see that religion wasn't enough. Her mama had religion, but it did nothing to save her. The boys who taunted her and Mama went to church every week, but they were still sinners, as were their fathers, including the one who visited Mama often.

- "If we confess our sins to [Jesus], he is faithful and just to forgive us our sins and to cleanse us from all wickedness"

(1 John 1:9). Once Angel believed in Jesus, she realized she needed to chart a new course. She couldn't go back to her old life, but she could trust God to lead her into a new one.

Who rescued Angel?

What role did Michael play in Angel's redemption?

Do you have more in common with Angel or Michael? How, and why?

3. The Bible is silent on the subject, but Hosea might have had doubts about redeeming Gomer from prostitution the second time. She had shamed him publicly. People knew he was a man of God, a prophet who spoke for God, yet his wife could be seen at the temple of Baal, offering fertility rites for a token sum. And she had children!

Hosea knew humiliation. He knew heartbreak. I'm sure there were times he closed his eyes and wished he could walk into the desert and never return to his hometown. Couldn't God use him someplace else?

But God had been explicit: "The LORD said to me, 'Go and love your wife again, even though she commits adultery with another lover. This will illustrate that the LORD still loves Israel, even though the people have turned to other gods and love to worship them'" (Hosea 3:1).

So Hosea obeyed, redeeming his wife and taking her back home, secure in the knowledge that what God had begun, God would finish. Gomer would forget about her lovers, confess her sin, and rejoice in her husband and children. Israel would forget about Baal, confess her sins, and rejoice in the Lord her God.

When did you realize you were a sinner? Were you a child? A teenager? An adult? After that realization, did you feel something drawing you toward God? If so, that was God at work. "No one can come to me," Jesus said, "unless the Father who sent me draws them to me, and at the last day I will raise them up" (John 6:44).

When you move toward God, confess your sins, and surrender your life to Him, He gives you a new life, a more abundant one in which you will never be alone.

Have you experienced the drawing of God? Have you taken the next step and surrendered your life? How has your life changed since then? What has God taught you? Where has He led you?

If you remain hesitant to surrender your life to Jesus, what holds you back from trusting Him? What would it take to remove those stumbling blocks?

4. Angel oversaw the House of Magdalena before she returned to Michael. Susanna Axle ran the home after that. Why do you think God allowed Angel to lead such a tragic life before she met Michael? What effect did Angel's past have on the girls at the House of Magdalena? Could it be that Angel's tears were seeds eventually sown in the lives of others? No one could speak as effectively to those young women as Angel because she had been where they were. She had felt what they were feeling.

What experiences in your life could God use or has He used to sow seeds in the lives of others? Write about them in your notebook.

5. What would have been lost if Michael had not obeyed the inner voice that told him to go visit Angel? How many lives would have been different?

What is lost when you ignore the voice of God when He speaks to you? He doesn't always speak audibly. Most of the time His voice is more of an inner nudge, a gentle push. What has He done in your life lately? How have you obeyed, and what happened as a result?

He will speak . . . if you will listen.

I hear the Savior say,
"Thy strength indeed is small.
Child of weakness, watch and pray.
Find in Me thine all in all."

Jesus paid it all!
All to Him I owe.
Sin had left a crimson stain;
He washed it white as snow.[20]

A FEW PARTING WORDS

A town once wished to honor one of its heroes, so they commissioned a sculptor to create a life-size statue of the man they desired to honor. When the statue arrived, however, "life-size" didn't seem grand enough, so they asked the sculptor to create a tall base to elevate the statue. The sculptor did, and the townspeople were happy—until someone pointed out that the statue was so high no one could see the fine details.

So the townspeople went to the sculptor once again. "One more thing," they said. "Can you create a miniature statue of our hero that we can place at eye level?"

That's what fiction is: it's an eye-level representation of universal truths. The people and events of the story may not be factual, but the underlying principles of good fiction are always true, and that's why they resonate with readers. That's why fiction can be more powerful than nonfiction.

I hope the story of Angel and Michael resonated in your heart and mind. I trust you will believe me when I say that though Angel and Michael are fictional characters, the God they talked about loves you as much as He loved them—and as much as He loves me. If you do not know Him, at this very moment He is waiting to hear from you.

Reach out to Him and trust His love. Turn from your old life, whatever it was, and let Him show you a new way of living. Like Angel, you can be reborn as a new person.

What are you waiting for?

NOTES

1. Glen MacDonough, "Toyland," *Babes in Toyland,* 1903, public domain.

2. William Ernest Henley, *Poems* (New York: Charles Scribner's Sons, 1922), 119.

3. See Oswald Chambers, "The Ethics of Enthusiasm," in *Biblical Ethics* (London: Marshall, Morgan & Scott, 1947).

4. Angela Ackerman and Becca Puglisi, *The Emotional Wound Thesaurus: A Writer's Guide to Psychological Trauma* (n.p.: Writers Helping Writers, 2017), 6.

5. John Donne, "Holy Sonnet 14," in *Seventeenth-Century Prose and Poetry,* ed. Alexander M. Witherspoon and Frank J. Warnke, 2nd ed. (New York: Harcourt, Brace & World, 1963), 757.

6. Gwen Purdie, *No More Hurting: Life Beyond Sexual Abuse* (Fearn, Scotland: Christian Focus, 2004), ebook.

7. "266. Hamartia," Bible Hub, accessed February 23, 2020, https://biblehub.com/greek/266.htm.

8. Elisabeth Elliot, *The Path of Loneliness: Finding Your Way Through the Wilderness to God* (Grand Rapids, MI: Revell, 2007), 123–24.

9. Lexico, s.v. "redemption," accessed February 24, 2020, www.lexico .com/en/definition/redemption.

10. Matthew Henry, *Matthew Henry's Commentary on the Whole Bible*, vol. 1, *Genesis to Deuteronomy* (Peabody, MA: Hendrickson, 1991), 112.

11. Johnson Oatman Jr., "Holy, Holy, Is What the Angels Sing," 1894, public domain.

12. David Guzik, "Study Guide for Hosea 1," Blue Letter Bible, 2001, www.blueletterbible.org/Comm/guzik_david/StudyGuide2017-Hsa /Hsa-1.cfm.

13. Guzik, "Study Guide."

14. Guzik, "Study Guide."

15. Wayne Grudem, *Systematic Theology: An Introduction to Biblical Doctrine* (Grand Rapids, MI: Zondervan, 1994), 442.

16. Grudem, *Systematic Theology*, 450.

17. Thomas Chisholm, "Great Is Thy Faithfulness," 1923, public domain.

18. Jackie DeShannon, "What the World Needs Now Is Love," by Hal David, *This Is Jackie DeShannon*, Capitol Records, 1965; The Beatles, "All You Need Is Love," by John Lennon, *Magical Mystery Tour*, Capitol Records, 1967; Deon Jackson, "Love Makes the World Go 'Round," *Love Makes the World Go 'Round*, Carla Records, 1966.

19. Adapted from Edward Herbert, *The Autobiography of Edward, Lord Herbert of Cherbury*, ed. Sidney L. Lee (London: John C. Nimmo, 1886), 63.

20. Elvina M. Hall, "Jesus Paid It All," 1865, public domain.